Housing Messages

COMMUNITY DEVELOPMENT SERIES

Series Editor: Richard P. Dober, AIP

URBAN ENVIRONMENTS AND HUMAN BEHAVIOR: An Annotated Bibliography/Edited by Gwen Bell et al.

DESIGNING FOR HUMAN BEHAVIOR: Architecture and the Behavioral Sciences/Edited by Jon Lang et al.

ALTERNATIVE LEARNING ENVIRONMENTS/Edited by Gary J. Coates

BEHAVIORAL RESEARCH METHODS IN ENVIRONMENTAL DESIGN/Edited by William Michelson

ARCHITECTURAL PSYCHOLOGY/Edited by Richard Kuller

MAN'S PERCEPTION OF MAN-MADE ENVIRONMENT/Sven Hesselgren

INSTRUCTIONAL MEDIA AND TECHNOLOGY: A Professional's Resource/Edited by Phillip J. Sleeman and D. M. Rockwell

NEIGHBORHOOD SPACE: User Needs and Design Responsibility/Randolph T. Hester

ENVIRONMENTAL KNOWING: Theories, Research, and Methods/Edited by Gary T. Moore and Reginald G. Golledge

PLANNING BUILDINGS AND FACILITIES FOR HIGHER EDUCATION/UNESCO

THE URBAN NEST/Anne-Marie Pollowy

DESIGNING THE OPEN NURSING HOME/Joseph A. Koncelik

METHODS OF ARCHITECTURAL PROGRAMMING/Henry Sanoff

HOUSING MESSAGES/Franklin D. Becker

EDRA Conference Publications

EDRA 1/Edited by Henry Sanoff and Sidney Cohn

EDRA 2/Edited by John Archea and Charles M. Eastman

ENVIRONMENTAL DESIGN RESEARCH, Vol. I: Selected Papers/Edited by Wolfgang F. E. Preiser (EDRA 4)

ENVIRONMENTAL DESIGN RESEARCH, Vol. II: Symposia and Workshops/Edited by Wolfgang F. E. Preiser (EDRA 4)

MAN-ENVIRONMENT INTERACTIONS: Evaluations and Applications, Parts I, II, and III/Edited by Daniel H. Carson (EDRA 5)

RESPONDING TO SOCIAL CHANGE/Edited by Basil Honikman (EDRA 6)

THE BEHAVIORAL BASIS OF DESIGN, BOOK 1/Edited by Peter Suedfeld and James A. Russell (EDRA 7)

CDS/30

Housing Messages

DISCARDED

Franklin D. Becker
CORNELL UNIVERSITY

ARTWORK BY
Janet Planet

Dowden, Hutchinson & Ross, Inc.
STROUDSBURG, PENNSYLVANIA

Copyright © 1977 by **Dowden, Hutchinson & Ross, Inc.**
Community Development Series, Volume 30
Library of Congress Catalog Card Number: 76-21267
ISBN: 0-87933-259-X

All rights reserved. No part of this book covered by the copyrights hereon may be reproduced or transmitted in any form or by any means—graphic, electronic, or mechanical, including photocopying, recording, taping, or information storage and retrieval systems—without written permission of the publisher.

77 78 79 5 4 3 2 1
Manufactured in the United States of America.

LIBRARY OF CONGRESS CATALOGING IN PUBLICATION DATA
Becker, Franklin D
   Housing messages.
   (Community development series ; v. 30)
   Includes index.
   1. Housing. 2. Architecture and society. 3. Nonverbal communication. 4. Social perception. I. Title
HD7287.5.B43   301.5'4   76-21267
ISBN 0-87933-259-X

To
Harriet and Bob

Series Editor's Foreword

By definition, the Community Development Series focuses on the diverse places that support human activities large and small. Communities range in scale from a family room to a metropolis. Within that spectrum, quantitatively, housing is the largest functional group of spaces. Accordingly, we welcome Franklin D. Becker's *Housing Messages.* It represents a single author's view about how physical forms themselves communicate certain values to those who see and use the physical environment, particularly human habitats.

Becker is well qualified to address the subject, having undertaken significant research on theory, as well as having pragmatic involvement with New York State's Urban Development Corporation when it was a large and adventuresome public agency constructing housing for all income groups on sites varied and comprehensive.

All those concerned with establishing housing policies and programs will thus immediately gain from Becker's work which lists many ideas and offers insights that can be translated into specific design responses. Whether or not significant amounts of new housing can be constructed these days when the median price unit is now $50,000.00 is a moot point. In that regard, those involved in rehabilitating the existing stock will find *Housing Messages* equally useful, especially since major problems exist that cry out for amelioration—problems of security, recreation, adequate social space.

In small and large ways, *Housing Messages* advances our editorial goals: to move planning and design issues from the rhetoric of good intentions into a state of action that will immediately benefit owners, users, and managers of the environment.

Richard P. Dober, AIP

Preface

Evaluating the built environment from the user's perspective has gradually become commonplace, at least in theory if not in practice. Postconstruction evaluation was spurred on initially by the repeated examples of classrooms, offices, pedestrian malls, and housing developments that failed to function as they were intended to by designers and administrators. Persons who became involved with postconstruction evaluation were struck by the obvious dysfunction of many buildings: doors opened in the wrong direction, bedrooms were too small to accommodate minimum furnishings, directional information was totally absent or misplaced and difficult to read, little consideration was given to children's play at different age levels. Satisfying activity requirements is one step toward creating more rewarding and habitable environments, but people are concerned about how things *look* as well as how they work, and often they cannot separate the two. The physical environment provides a set of cues that people interpret in different ways and that they use as a basis for making inferences about what activities are appropriate, how others treat them, and how they think and want others to think about themselves.

The real estate, advertising, and marketing professions have long understood that peoples' purchasing behavior is closely tied to products as symbols of status, intelligence, power, and sophistication. The design professions know this also, but they have traditionally interpreted their role in providing consumer products as an elevating or uplifting one; they want to change popular tastes, not cater to them. This book is predicated on the assumption that the role of the design professions is not as "taste-changers" but as "image-tappers," creating products and buildings whose images are in some way connected to peoples' feelings, aspirations, and experiences.

Chapter 1 describes the role of the physical environment as a communication medium; chapters 2 and 3 look at some of the images people have of housing environments and how public housing generally reflects the values of those who create it; chapters 4 and 5 address the question of *who* should or can create appropriate images for a setting's occupants, by what processes, and for whose benefit; chapters 6, 7, and 8 discuss environmental messages associated with specific components of the housing environment and how the inferences made on the basis of physical cues can help generate or dissipate conflict between individuals and groups; chapter 9 discusses the use of the physical environment as part of a social change process.

Many people contributed to this book directly and indirectly. The support of Theodore Liebman, Jim Wiley, and Doug Wonderlic was especially appreciated while I was doing the research for the *Design for Living* report, which I cite frequently in this book. Lawrence Friedberg and Tasuku Ohazama were also invaluable in making that report possible. Jean Shorett, Mark Saxer, Janet Planet, Steve Cohen, Abe Wandersman, and Sharon Davidoff provided many ideas and critical comments on earlier drafts of this book. Harriet Becker and Robert Sommer have contributed over many years in far too many ways to indicate here. I am indebted to them for their ideas and support.

Portions of this book have appeared in modified form in the *Journal of Housing, Journal of Architectural Research, Humanitas,* and *Design for Living: The Residents' View of Multifamily Housing.*

Franklin D. Becker

Contents

Series Editor's Foreword   vii

Preface   ix

1 Environmental Messages   1

2 Images of Home   15

3 Public Housing   37

4 Personalization   51

5 Participation   71

6 Vandalism and Crime   89

7 Children's Play   107

8 Housing Management   119

9 Social Change   129

Index   139

Housing Messages

1
Environmental Messages

> We all consciously look for nonverbal clues in buildings, landscapes, and interiors, for we know that these clues have something to say about the status, prestige, and other values of those who own them.
>
> J. Ruesch and W. Kees, *Nonverbal Communication*[1]

From fur coats and cars, jewelry and houses, hair styles and hair length, recreation vehicles and cameras, we infer that people are intelligent, warm, creative, wealthy, trustworthy, and solid citizens—or poor, untrustworthy, weak, and immoral. We use these same physical cues to measure our own identity and self-esteem. Initially ice hockey players refused to wear protective head gear because they felt it reflected a lack of courage and diminished the "toughness" of their sport. Elderly persons have preferred uncomfortable chairs to ones designed especially for them because the "better" chairs were institutional looking. Low-income parents have had a playground built by their children with surplus materials razed because it was made of "junk" and symbolized second-class citizenship to them.

Creating buildings and interior spaces that are functional—they meet government codes for safety and sanitation, or they allow certain transactions to be fulfilled with the minimum of effort, or they "work" in the sense that a stove will heat water or brakes will stop a car—is absolutely necessary—and insufficient. To create environments that not only "work" but that *will be used* and are rewarding to those who inhabit and use them, designers must understand the kinds of associations different people make to buildings, furniture, and other design elements and how these associations and interpretations of

Housing Messages

physical cues affect peoples' feelings of self-esteem, their social standing in the community, and their relationships to their family, friends, and neighbors.

This book explores the social and psychological implications of common physical cues—the kind and quality of materials used in a building, the level of maintenance, the shape of a roof, the arrangement of dwelling units—as symbols of status, competency, respectability, identity, caring, and other everyday concerns.

Design of all types—graphics, interior, architecture, product—has long emphasized the way in which the selection and arrangement of particular images and associations affects people's attitudes and behavior. But design, in the sense of creating images through the manipulation of space, materials, and objects, is not the sole prerogative of experts such as architects. Most people are designers in the sense that they *send* their own environmental messages through their use, selection, and arrangement of objects, furnishings, and space. In a pluralistic society where there is no single unifying set of values, philosophy, or religion (with the possible exception of personal economic gain), the physical environment, as a reflection of an underlying social organization, inevitably presents contrasting and conflicting images. The kinds of conflicts E. T. Hall has described as a consequence of misinterpretation of nonverbal attitudes communicated through body position and distance may be occurring around us every day as a function of misinterpretation of nonverbal messages communicated through the physical environment;[2] or, ironically, as a result of agreement about *what* the environmental messages are, but with the social meaning and impact on the groups or individuals associated with the environmental message being very different than it is for groups who may form their identity by *not* being associated with the same physical cues.

Consciously and unconsciously we interpret our physical environment in a variety of ways. We try to understand the motivations and intentions of those who designed it, the ways in which it affects our behavior and influences our emotional reactions, and what its symbolic meaning is within a particular context. Lee Rainwater describes this type of meta-message with respect to public housing:

> The physical evidence of trash, poor plumbing, and the stink that goes with it, rats and other

Environmental Messages 3

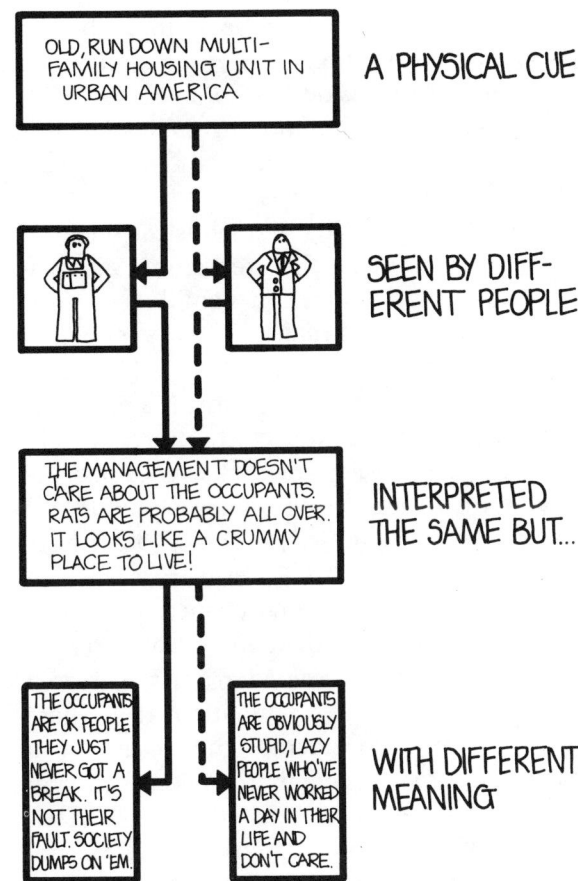

vermin, deepen their feelings of being moral outcasts. Their physical world is telling them that they are inferior and bad just as effectively perhaps as do their human interactions.[3]

The discrepancy in values between those who authorize, plan, and design the buildings and those who live in and use them is often tremendous in public housing. More affluent segments of the housing market have the opportunity to select from a number of alternatives those that best reflect and enhance their own sense of worth and identity; or, if they buy a home, they can modify it in a way that reflects their own perceived image and self-esteem. Users of public housing and other residential institutions such as dormitories, hospitals, and prisons have many fewer options, and generally they must make do with what they are provided by government or nonprofit private agencies.

Public housing like mental institutions, dormitories, prisons, and other residential institutions managed by one group for the "good" of another can be characterized by the generally paternalistic and negative images they convey to their inhabitants and the occupants' feelings of being neglected, ignored, and treated impersonally. In the context of a therapeutic environment for autistic children, Bruno Bettelheim has written of the importance of what he calls "silent messages," which convey through the minute details of the physical environment the staff's concern for the patients' well-being. He makes the point, often overlooked by designers and administrators concerned with the overall design or form of a building, that an institution's intentions are conveyed by the smallest details of the staff's behavior and the physical environment. The occupants spend a great deal of time trying to interpret the staff's attitudes toward them, given in the form of these nonverbal messages. Bettelheim describes autistic children who have a poor opinion of their body and the way it functions and the importance of the bathroom in demonstrating to these patients, nonverbally through its furnishings, the esteem the staff and institutions hold of his or her body. Bettelheim feels that eventually patients may be able to model their feelings for the body's worthwhileness, and on this basis their self-respect, on the image of it conveyed through the bathroom design and furnishings.[4]

Just as mental patients are often surrounded by conditions and exposed to messages telling them that the administrators of the environment in which they live expect—and hence fear—that they may act destructively (by locked doors, for instance), so do public-housing projects with their hard finishes and supposedly indestructible surfaces and lack of amenities convey the administration's lack of trust in the residents.

Ruesch and Kees have called attempts to influence without words "object language" and defined it as "all intentional and nonintentional displays of material things, such as implements, machines, art objects, architectural structures, and—last but not least—the human body, and whatever clothes or covers it."[5] The material aspects of words, and the style and substance of the letters and numerals, also function symbolically. Polished bronze numerals on a solid oak door signify something different about the inhabitants of that space, and the way they wish to be perceived than does a scrawled sign on a cracked and peeling plywood door. We use these object symbols to set the scene for social encounters. Ruesch and Kees note that in a democracy, where all individuals are equal, objects have the useful function of announcing inequality that "for reason of taste and conformity, cannot be expressed in words.... These hazards may be circumvented by the use of object language, which can operate 24 hours a day, is accessible to both rich and poor, literate and illiterate, and may be visible at a considerable distance." Vance Packard became famous chronicling how Americans attempt to differentiate themselves from their neighbors through the purchase of cars, homes, clothes, appliances, and other "extensions of our personality" in a never-ending attempt to enhance status relative to their neighbors, or to at least "keep up with the Joneses."[6]

The way in which the physical environment can symbolically represent management's attitudes toward employees was unexpectedly illustrated in an industrial context many years ago in a study widely known as the Hawthorne study (named after the location where the study occurred). In 1939 Roethlisberger and Dickson studied the effects of different environmental conditions on worker productivity. They found that productivity increased linearly, regardless of the type of environmental change. Increasing lighting increased productivity, as did decreasing lighting. Providing piped-in music increased productivity as did eliminating it.[7] These findings were considered the result of a faulty research design that failed to control for spurious effects, and the term "Hawthorne effect" is now used to describe observed changes in behavior and attitudes that are a function of uncontrolled (and sometimes unknown) variables. Robert Sommer has suggested that rather than demonstrating the spurious effects of environmental changes, the study demonstrated the fallacy of a simple deterministic model of behavior.[8] The environmental changes did make a difference, but their effect was a function of the ways in which individuals interpreted these changes and the significance they attributed to them. Seeing is believing, and the concrete evidence that management was concerned about the employees' environment conveyed positive attitudes of the management toward its employees in a way that words could not. Through the changes in the environmental conditions, management unintentionally reinforced the employees' own sense of worth and value.

SELF-CONCEPT AND PHYSICAL OBJECTS AS SYMBOLS

The notion that individuals define, reinforce, and extend their sense of self through the acquisition and display of physical objects is not new. At the turn of the century, William James, writing about sources of self-esteem, defined the self as

> the sum total of all that he can call his, not only his body and his psychic processes, but his clothes and his house, his wife and children, his ancestors and his friends, his reputation and works, his lambs and horses, his yacht and bank account. All things give him the same emotions. If they wax and prosper, he feels "triumphant"; if they dwindle and die away, he feels cast down—not necessarily in the same degree for each thing, but in much the same way for all.[9]

Strauss has written that a man's possessions are a fair index of what he is, providing the observers take the trouble to distinguish what a man owns by chance and to what he is really endeared.[10] He notes that it is no accident that men mark their symbolic movements—from one social class to another, for instance—by discarding old clothes, houses, furnishings, friends, even wives. The significance of possessions and properties is often revealed by reactions to their loss: people not only lose their property but also their sense of direction and purpose in life.

Vance Packard[11] and William H. Whyte[12] have also noted the "object value" that a spouse, cars, homes, and addresses have for corporation executives and how the extent and kind of these "objects" can influence an executive's career and advancement. These possessions become public symbols of and represent one's values, status, and degree of success and, as such, both inform others of one's identity and, at the same time, reinforce one's own sense of self.

Although the judgment of our self-esteem and our identity may be subjective and personal, it develops through our interactions with others and is highly influenced by others' impressions of us and their reactions to our behavior and our values as expressed, often to a large extent, by displays of possessions.

Within the above context, goods of a variety of sorts, from automobiles to homes, can be viewed as "social tools" or symbols that function both as a means of communication among individuals and as a significant reference. Our possessions, as much as our gestures and body orientation and social distance, are a form of nonverbal communication that represents us to others in particular ways. They are symbols, things that stand for or suggest something else. They may do this by reason of relationship, association, convention, even accident; but for any kind of an object to serve as a symbol, it must have a shared meaning for at least two people and for all the people with whom one desires to communicate.

In effect, the process of developing shared meanings is a classification process where

6   Housing Messages

objects are placed in relation to other objects. The meaning of things lies in the perspective, not in the thing, and the way in which things are classed together reveals the perspective of the classifier.[13] By defining what the object is, we arouse a set of expectations toward the object and those associated with it, and these expectations function as a guide or prescription for appropriate behavior.

Fraternity initiation rites where new members are forced to eat "worms" that are, in fact, cold spaghetti are a vivid example of how our reactions to an object are conditioned by our classification of it. The same object may have very different meanings for different individuals or groups, eliciting negative reactions where positive ones were anticipated. We project our understandings of a meaning of a possession or an activity onto others, and when the definitions of meaning only partially overlap, misunderstanding and conflict are imminent.

SYMBOLS AND ENVIRONMENTAL DESIGN

When symbols have been considered in relationship to environmental design, the discussion has usually been restricted to the analysis of monumental buildings and to special buildings within this tradition, particularly religious and civic. The importance of symbols in the Byzantine church seen as icon, the mosque and its court in Iran as symbol of paradise, and the Roman pantheon as the ideal dome of heaven are well recognized, but we know much less about the symbolism and meaning of ordinary architecture.[14] Most studies of symbolism are distinguished by the focus on a special *place* that is distinguished from the spaces around it. These studies do not attempt to analyze other forms of organized space that are more utilitarian in character than the frequently scrutinized churches and public buildings. Yet artifacts, including buildings and settlements, are one way of making concrete the immaterial nature of values and norms of a society.[15] What becomes significant in a study of building form and function as types of environmental messages is that the buildings may be expressing a set of values and objectives different from and inconsistent with those held by the persons inhabiting the space, however congruent they may be with those held by that part of society responsible for creating these structures.

Given our penchant for studying the past, the distant, and the exotic, it is not surprising that we are more aware of how buildings in primitive culture express underlying values and beliefs than we are about the same processes in our own society. For example, writing about cultural influences on house forms, Rapoport suggests that for the Dogon and Bambara tribes of Mali every object and social event has a symbolic as well as a utilitarian function.

> Houses, household objects, and chairs all have this symbolic quality, and the Dogon civilization, otherwise relatively poor, has several thousand symbolic elements. The frame plots and whole landscape of the Dogon reflect this cosmic order. Their villages are built in pairs to represent heaven and earth, and fields are cleared in spirals because the world has been created spirally. The villages are laid out in the way parts of the body lie with respect to each other, while the house of the Dogon, or paramount sheath, is a model of the universe as a smaller scale. Multi-storied houses are the prerogative of the highest religious and political leaders and are symbols of power, representations of them being used for many purposes; for example, as masks frighten away the soul of the dead.[16]

The forms of buildings become signs that reflect the preconceptions of those who determined them, with these forms reflecting the inner life, actions, and social conceptions of the occupants. The social meaning of a building becomes understandable only within what Gregor Paulsson has described as their "symbol milieu," where all objects gain meaning and are interpreted in the context of their association with human actions and values.[17]

In the earliest civilizations, for example, it was impossible to distinguish between practical and religious (magical) meanings. The first permanent huts in Sumer were built by bending rushes without removing the roots from the ground. The rushes were tied together at the top, and arches formed in this way were connected with horizontal sticks. The resulting hut had its roots in the ground and hence was unified with the element from which life gets its nourishment. These primitive building forms resulted from the need for protection, and physical, as well as social and cultural, aspects were unified in this need. These first huts offered protection against a capricious and dangerous physical environment, provided security by being a visual expression of the group, and at the same time protected against hostile forces by collaborating with the life-giving forces.[18]

The same process of differentiation and cultural symbolization occurs currently, but with the type of meaning of the symbols specific to our culture and particular groups within it. Places of work generally reflect not only their functional purpose but are differentiated according to underlying concepts and values. Hospitals must not only meet certain sanitation criteria; they must also *appear* to be clean and sanitary. The image of the hospital and healing can be as important a healing element as the level of skill and knowledge actually available. A design office that does not appear "architectonic" may lessen a potential customer's confidence in the firm's architectural skills. Our buildings may lack religious symbolism, but we are not a very religious society. We are a consumer-oriented, status-conscious society, and if we look for symbols representing these values, goals, and aspirations, we are likely to find them. Symbolism in environmental design is alive; it simply is so much around us we take it for granted.

SYMBOLISM IN ORDINARY ARCHITECTURE

By ordinary architecture, I mean buildings that are intended for common uses by the general public. These can include institutions, such as schools and dormitories, as well as public multifamily housing developments and single-family detached houses. The definition excludes buildings intended to be monumental, such as museums, civic buildings, and many churches. Most ordinary buildings are designed by nonarchitects, although not all of them. Le Pessac, a housing development designed by Le Corbusier in France, is ordinary architecture by the above definition because it was not intentionally monumental and it is used by common people for ordinary purposes.[19] It is symbolic, however, in that the modern design, typified by the flat roofs uncharacteristic of that region of France, were deliberately representative of a new industrial era and were consciously intended to break with tradition. Levittown is also ordinary architecture within this definition, with as explicit a symbolism as Le Corbusier's but following a very different direction: it attempts to reflect current and traditional values and images of "home" rather than creating new images. Much of ordinary architecture, like schools, incorporates no *deliberate* symbolism and is considered almost purely functional. Yet the most functional buildings and environments can be highly symbolic, often in undesired and unexpected ways.

Interior space planning involving the selection and arrangement of furnishings is another example of how the physical environment is used to reflect underlying social norms and values by conveying messages about status, leadership, and appropriate role behavior. Sommer found that when visitors to a hospital setting were given free choice in sitting at rectangular tables that the leader of the group would take the seat at the head of the table, and the other participants would sit as close to the leader as possible.[20] These results are similar to Strodbeck and Hook's findings in a study of jury behavior that the person who sat at the head of the table was likely to be a person of managerial or executive rank; thus, existing leadership roles were reflected and reinforced by particular seating positions.[21] Sitting at the head of the table or standing at the front of the lecture room may make comfortable conversation difficult and increase the distance between the leader and other participants, but this symbolizes the differences among the participants and can be a positive attribute of the arrangement for those interested in maintaining role and status distinctions. The desire by others to eliminate such arrangements simply reveals how the values and perspectives of the observer affect the interpretation of physical cues.

The possibility of the same symbol, or manifestations of that symbol, being differently interpreted by groups with dissimilar values is, of course, constantly occurring. Architects and nonprofessionals, respectively, find single-family "ranch" houses either in "poor taste" or the perfect home. As Vance Packard says, the house advertised as "Early American Luxurious Ranch" is in Long Island, not the Texas panhandle.[22] People buy symbols. Most designers do not really quarrel with the symbol but with its lack of authenticity. People *without* recourse to an authentic Italian villa or genuine farmhouse still want a home that reinforces the status image they wish to project of themselves, and they can succeed if their audience consists of other persons like themselves who are, in a sense, also pretending. The accelerating market in "original" oil paintings produced in factories according to formula and available in a choice of colors reflects people's desire to share in the status of being able to patronize the arts.[23]

Those who can afford authentic original art and can recognize the difference between it and what they perceive as "schlock" art may feel that hanging an inexpensive reproduction of a "real" artist may be in better taste than displaying "factory" paintings, but those who buy "schlock" art are pleasing themselves and impressing their friends, not persons they only read about. Packard quotes a *Chicago Tribune* reporter who summed up the attitude toward houses: "You have to *look* successful. A house is a very tangible symbol of success... and the residence is regarded as a goal and a symbol, as well as something to live in."[24]

People who can afford them will buy antiques and original paintings; those who cannot will buy imitations. What becomes symbolic for those with the cash and the training is authenticity itself, and so architects and designers are continually found in restored old farmhouses and gristmills. The spaces are ample and pleasant, and so is the image of understanding quality and being creative and inventive enough to see the beauty in what others may have discarded. Among other groups of people *seemingly* mundane accessories and "features" are employed to help create desired images: air conditioners (when they were a novelty), television aerials (also when they were a novelty), certain types of fences, hedges, circular driveways—the list could go on and on. All of these objects have one characteristic in common: they proclaim to oneself, friends, and passers-by one's status, values, and tastes.

Even the most trivial and mundane objects can acquire the status of meaningful symbols, and they can have an important influence on people's perceptions, attitudes, and behavior. To design homes, or any other type of building, without attempting to understand the kinds of symbols that elicit desired reactions, rather than negative ones, and the range of people for whom these symbols are meaningful is to ignore a fundamental component of people's evaluations of buildings, objects, and urban landscapes. Yet this is what most institutional buildings, including public housing, dormitories, prisons, and offices, do.

In part, the failure of much of modern architecture to incorporate symbols that elicit the intended reactions can be related to the distinction, first made by Gibson, between the perceptual and associational worlds.[25] Gibson proposed a hierarchy of levels of meaning, ranging from concrete meanings—the ground, for instance—to activity-oriented meaning—the ground as something to be walked upon—through value and other meanings to the extreme of symbolic meaning—the ground as homeland. The perception of an object becomes more and more culturally determined as it possesses higher levels of meaning, and these meanings are learned, not given in the object themselves.

While the concrete and use meaning of objects and environments is shared by a wide variety of people, the higher levels of meaning are more personal and less predictable. Manipulating high-level meanings, those in the associational world, is extremely difficult compared to achieving lower-level meanings. We can build walls that everyone will recognize as barriers of sorts, but the meaning of these barriers, or even the association made to particular materials used to construct the walls, may differ considerably among different people. An expensive apartment complex designed by an internationally known architect has "unfinished" poured-concrete ceilings that reveal the framing and nails used to mold them. Some people cannot understand why they should pay high rent for a building that is not, and will never be "finished." Similarly, the housing development Le Corbusier designed in Le Pessac in France has been remodeled almost beyond recognition by successive generations of tenants who found the original flat roofs unsupportive of their notion of a proper house, and so changed them to the sloping roofs traditional in that region.[26] It is conceivable that the architect in both instances could have learned about these particular associations, shared by large segments of the population, before designing the buildings. In other cases it is not so easy. Associations change with time. Americans, in particular, have a tendency to reevaluate the meaning and desirability of buildings and structures rather rapidly. Old factories and warehouses that were considered eyesores and financial liabilities twenty years ago have within the past few years become valued for

Environmental Messages   11

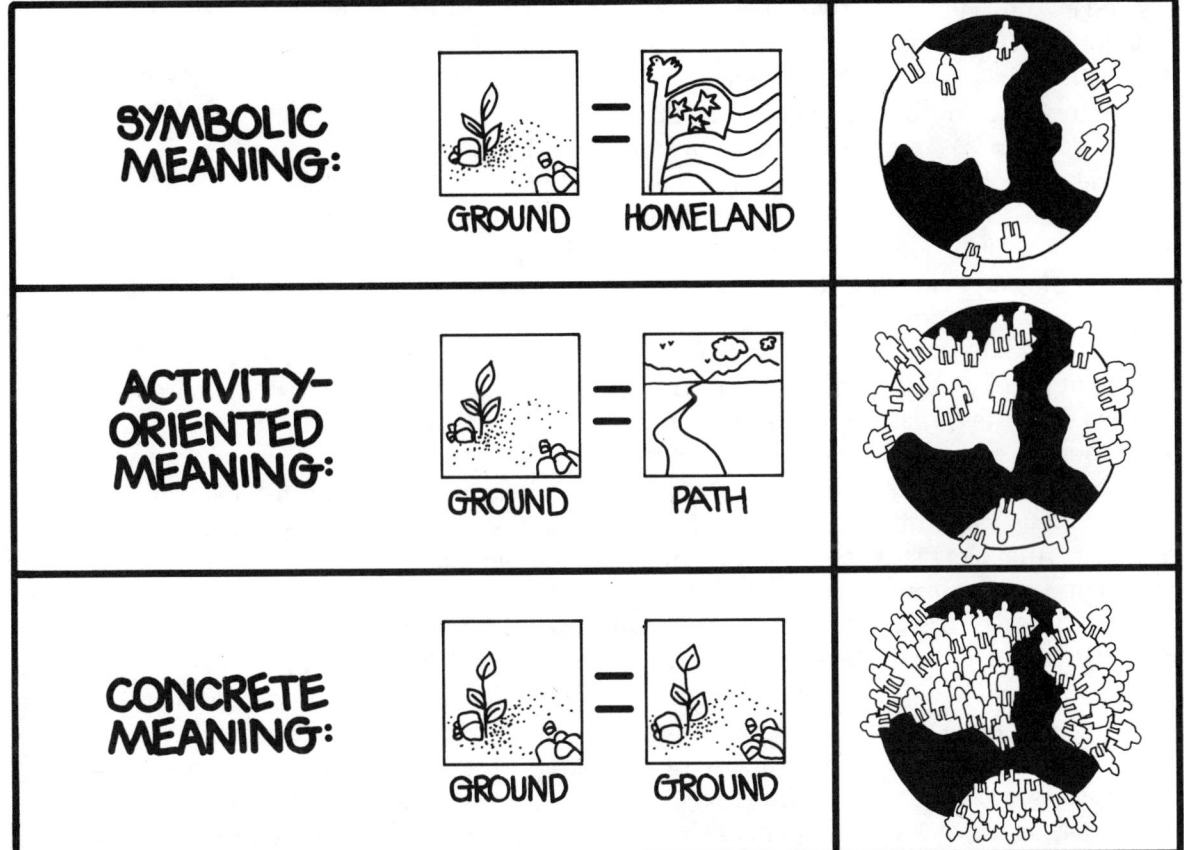

their strength, beauty of construction, and their history and have been restored and renovated into useful and highly successful shopping and business ventures.

The continuous change in the meaning and use of the same structures, as well as the creation of new buildings whose form expresses no particular function, has resulted in banks that look like colonial homes, restaurants that look like gas stations (and were before they were renovated), gas stations that look like city halls, and apartment complexes that look like insurance buildings. This state of affairs contrasts sharply with primitive and "vernacular" architecture, where form and symbolic meaning are congruent; as a consequence, the environment is "legible"—it provides cues for expected behavior.[27] People know what behaviors are expected of them—what to wear, what to say, who is allowed in, and what services they can expect.

Vernacular architecture is characterized by a standard design "model" in which minor variations are allowed but in which what Boyd has called "featurism"—where the major stress is on differences and "features"—does not exist.[28] Ironically, some of the most despised buildings (by architects) and the most liked buildings (food?) by nonarchitects are chain food establishments (for example, MacDonald's hamburgers), which are similar to traditional vernacular architecture in that the models used are totally consistent (look for the golden arch). Such building forms may make concrete some ideal (as Rapoport suggests design should), which involves the matching and evaluation of the physical design against an image of what is desirable. Architects such as Robert Venturi and Denise Scott Brown have gone as far as to promote these urban "vernacular" images as a basis for a new design aesthetic.[29]

As a means of avoiding the global implications of a concept like *image* and making its relationship to design more operational, Rapoport suggests dealing with *specifics*, which may allow us to get at differences in images and life-styles by starting with simpler, more molecular concepts, such as activities and (in architecture), functions. Rapoport uses cooking as an example. Any activity—eating, shopping, playing—can be divided into four components: (1) the activity proper; (2) a specific way of doing it; (3) additional, adjacent, or associated activities that become part of an activity system; and (4) symbolic aspects of the activity.

The activity is one of converting raw food into cooked. The specific way may involve frying, roasting, or other means, the use of special kinds of utensils or ovens, squatting on the floor, etc. Associated activities may include socializing, exchanging information, listening to music, etc. The symbolic meaning of cooking may be ritual, a way of acquiring status, a way of asserting some special social identity or membership in a group.

It is the difference in these four aspects of apparently simple activities and functions which lead to specific forms of settings, differences in their relative importance, the amount of time spent in them, who was involved, etc.—in fact, all the kinds of things which affect design and form.[30]

It is the variability of the last two elements of the activity, the associated activities and the symbolic aspect, that leads to different physical forms. Groups may engage in the same activities, but because of the image of these activities and the meanings associated with them, different groups may consider some locations more appropriate than others for these activities and make inferences about people on the basis of *where* they engage in certain activities. For example, many middle-class men repair their own cars as do lower-class men, but middle-class men are generally able to engage in this hobby in the privacy of their garage, invisible to the public. Lower-class men generally do not have garages and so work on the street, in full public view and often with associated social activities being an important component of the activity. Use of public areas for such hobbies/social gatherings has different meanings for middle-class groups who feel such activities are appropriately done out of public view and may lead to negative labeling of one group or area by the other—"lower class," "slums"—and social conflict among groups.

Tenants in architect-designed apartments who personalize exterior spaces like porches and backyards with the materials and artifacts of their choosing (linoleum with brick pattern, for instance) may incur the wrath of management or disdain of nonresidents for whom such displays convey images of "bad taste" and "lower class." For the resident, they may convey completely opposite images of "home," "pride," and "belonging."[31]

We need to understand the meaning and associations different groups attach to different materials, artifacts, and physical arrangements and how these meanings support their own sense of self and identity. The design professions and the public generally have different images and evaluate environments differently, and within the public there are an almost infinite number of groups with different images. Yet although there are different images held by different groups, we need to explore the possibility that there are some basic images that are central to all groups. Pitched roofs, front and back distinctions, and extensive landscaping may be concepts that are universally accepted as desirable even if particular expressions are different. If the validity of such concepts can be established and incorporated into any design solution that is created, leaving the particular embellishment or "style" of the expression to the individual tastes of the occupants, the design may be more successful than it has been in the recent past.

The following chapters examine some of the images and associations different groups, particularly low- and moderate-income residents in public multifamily housing, hold of their environment and how their interpretation of "environmental messages" affects their sense of self-esteem and their attitudes toward their neighbors and management. It should become clear that people are not passive recipients of messages sent to them by others. They are active participants in structuring their own worlds. They use the physical environment to express their own values, attitudes, tastes, and identity.

REFERENCES

1. J. Ruesch and W. Kees, *Nonverbal Communication: Notes on the Visual Perception of Human Relations* (Berkeley, Calif.: University of California Press, 1956).
2. E. T. Hall, *The Silent Language* (New York: Doubleday & Company, 1959). See also V. Packard, *The Hidden Persuaders* (New York: Pocket Books, 1957).
3. L. Rainwater, "Fear and the House-as-Haven in the Lower Class," *Journal of the American Institute of the Planners* 32 (1956): 23-37.
4. B. Bettelheim, *Home for the Heart* (New York: Bantam Books, 1974).
5. Ruesch and Kees, *Nonverbal Communication.*
6. V. Packard, *The Status Seekers* (New York: David McKay Co., 1959).
7. J. F. Roethlisberger and W. J. Dickson, *Management and the Worker* (Cambridge: Harvard University Press, 1939).
8. R. Sommer, "Hawthorne Dogma," *Psychological Bulletin* 70 (1968): 592-598.
9. W. James, *Principles of Psychology* (New York: Holt, 1890), cited by S. Coopersmith, *The Antecedents of Self-Esteem* (San Francisco: W. H. Freeman and Company, 1967).
10. A. Strauss, *Mirrors and Masks: The Search for Identity* (Glencoe, Ill.: The Free Press, 1959).

11. Packard, *The Status Seekers*.
12. W. H. Whyte, *Organization Man* (New York: Doubleday & Company, 1956).
13. Strauss, *Mirrors and Masks*.
14. See A. Rapoport, "Symbolism and Environmental Design," *International Journal of Symbology* 1 (1970): 1-9. See also A. Rapoport, "Images, Symbols, and Popular Design," *International Journal of Symbology* 4 (1973): 1-12.
15. P. A. Sorokin, *Society Culture and Personality* (New York: Harper, 1947), cited by Rapoport, *House Form and Culture*.
16. A. Rapoport, *House Form and Culture* (Englewood Cliffs, N.J.: Prentice-Hall, 1969).
17. G. Paulsson, *The Study of Cities* (Kobenhavn, 1959), cited by C. Norberg-Schulz, *Intentions in Architecture* (Rome: Universitetsforlaget, 1963).
18. C. Norberg-Schulz, *Intentions in Architecture* (Rome: Universitetsforlaget, 1963).
19. P. Boudon, *Lived-In Architecture* (Cambridge: The MIT Press, 1969).
20. R. Sommer, "Small Group Ecology," *Psychological Bulletin* 67 (1967): 145-152.
21. F. L. Strodtbeck and L. Hook, "The Social Dimensions of a Twelve Man Jury Table," *Sociometry* 24 (1961): 397-415.
22. Packard, *The Status Seekers*.
23. D. Black, "Schlock Art—'For $2.50 You Don't Get Dewdrops,'" *The New York Times,* May 11, 1975.
24. Packard, *The Status Seekers*.
25. J. J. Gibson, *The Perception of the Visual World* (Boston: Houghton Mifflin, 1950), cited by Rapoport, "Symbolism and Environmental Design."
26. Boudon, *Lived-In Architecture*.
27. Rapoport, *House Form and Culture*.
28. Ibid.
29. R. Venturi, D. Brown, and S. Izenour, *Learning from Las Vegas* (Cambridge: The MIT Press, 1972).
30. Rapoport, *House Form and Culture*.
31. F. D. Becker, *Design for Living: The Residents' View of Multifamily Housing* (Ithaca, N.Y.: Center for Urban Development Research, Cornell University, 1974).

2

Images of Home

> The dream home is surrounded by trees and grass in either country or suburb, and must be *owned,* yet Americans rarely stay in it more than five years. It is not a real need but a symbol . . . . The ideal of home is esthetic, not functional.
>
> R. Cramer, *"Images of Home"*[1]

If a study by William Michelson is accurate, the image of "home" and the meanings associated with it cannot at the present time be adequately represented by multifamily housing, at least in the United States. Michelson found that 85 percent of a sample of nearly 700 Americans, randomly selected by stage in life cycle, socioeconomic status, and present living situation, preferred living in single-family houses.[2] Since two-thirds of the people living in multifamily housing also preferred living in single-family houses, it is difficult to support the old adage that people like what they have. The fact that 91 percent of young couples without children and 84 percent of older couples without children preferred single-family houses challenges the conventional wisdom that only young couples with children really want single-family houses. The assumption that it is the economic advantages of home ownership that account for the preference for single-family houses was placed in doubt when only 2 percent of those who preferred single-family houses changed their minds and said they preferred multifamily living when condominiums were presented as an alternative to renting or home ownership. Making multifamily housing more functional as a means of increasing its acceptance may be logical—and unsuccessful.

Utility and convenience may be deliberately sacrificed for "image" considerations related to social prestige, particularly in economies of scarcity. In Peru, when the walls of a house in the barriada are finished, the rooms are usually roofed with cane, the windows bricked up, and cement floors put in. When more money is earned, the first purchase is a large elaborate cedar door; once the door and wooden windows are installed, the people feel like owners.[3] The status symbol of the door takes precedence over the utility of keeping out rain and cold. Among the rural poor in upstate New York a color television or snowmobile may be purchased before a septic system or well. For the rural poor in particular, the single-family dwelling—whether it be a dilapidated farmhouse, a trailer, a converted bus—remains the preferred dwelling type. This preference, however, is as much a function of its location "on the outside," which makes surveillance by social workers and enforcement of building codes difficult, and the small initial investment to own the residence, which obviates making monthly payments, as it is of the type of dwelling unit itself.[4]

Among young people in this country seeking alternative life-styles to suburban living, the image of home as a free-standing dwelling unit often remains, but utility is defined in terms of ecological relationships where the use of recycled windows, doors, and plumbing is a means of visually demonstrating a set of values in opposition to unlimited energy consumption and waste of raw materials. The definition of utilitarian changes from lack of frills, concern with efficiency, and desire for energy-consuming, "labor-saving" devices to an emphasis on energy-saving recycling of materials, craftsmanship, and the "beauty" of a home expressing individual tastes, life-styles, and values.

In many ways the new hand-built houses embody characteristics of buildings found in early New England. The original New England houses were built on an oak frame using the simplest tools and were an intricate piece of carpentry. The house was neither painted nor adorned, but the years of weathering gave it a natural beauty. In comparison to contemporary standards of utility, these houses were nonfunctional: the huge chimney was inefficient and the lighting in the house was poor. Yet these "inefficiencies" were, in fact, highly utilitarian. Few windows made heating the house easier and more economical, and the fireplace was a stove, heater, and symbol of "home" simultaneously. Harsh winters and the lack of mobility made the expenditure of time and energy for detailed and solid construction and craftsmanship worthwhile. The plan of the house reflected the social system. The ground floor had two main rooms—a combination living room-work room-kitchen with a large fireplace and a parlor that was reserved for important guests and family religious observances. Between these two rooms a flight of stairs led to the two bedrooms where the family slept, and above these, reached by a ladder, was the attic where the servant slept.[5]

The house sheltered the economic and biological functions of the domestic life of the family, but the social and cultural functions belonged to the meetinghouse. It was here that discussion of civic affairs took place, where weapons and ammunition were stored, and where community celebrations were held. The community house was the center of social life because the community was the heart of existence. These early American communities provided as a matter of course the type of social organization many people are attempting to recreate today, but with less structuring of roles and without the rigid status hierarchies found in early New England that prescribed what people wore and in what activities they could engage.

The early New England type of social organization, and the houses and community structures that supported it, were gradually replaced with houses scattered throughout vast geographical areas, where the family unit became the basic social and economic unit, with the community more a marketplace than a superfamily. The house reflected its new social function, as well as the recognition that one's family would change in size and economic resources over time and might even move to another house. Houses were built that could be easily sold, and so they would be flexible to changes over time. Balloon construction involving the substitution of thin plates and studs running the entire height of the building and held together by nails was substituted for the more expensive and time-consuming method of construction with mortised and tenoned joints. The house was inexpensive and fast to build and more convenient than the earlier New England houses. Unlike earlier houses, which were planned to accommodate prescribed social functions and hierarchies—a room for ceremonies, one for the family, one for the servant—these houses were planned more in terms of practical functions: kitchen, milkroom, pantry, living room, bedroom. The most important room was dedicated to family gatherings rather than ceremonial occasions and reflected the new self-sufficiency of families. The family house supplanted the community house as a symbol of social cohesion.[6]

This type of house, in turn, was supplanted by houses where family life took the form of eating meals together, or watching television or listening to the radio, but where the family as a unit, particularly a self-sufficient economic group, was replaced by distant places of work, learning, and leisure. Even simpler forms of construction (concrete block, for instance) were substituted for the more intricate balloon-frame construction, and the advent of electric, gas, and oil heating made the fireplaces and hearths functionally unnecessary. Yet it is significant that although the function and meaning of houses has changed over time, reflecting changes in family and community structure, the central image of a *freestanding* dwelling unit has remained, and many "features" that are no longer necessities, such as fireplaces, are still incorporated into houses because they support the image of "home" and hearth in houses that otherwise may elicit few positive associations. At least in America, Britain, and much of Western Europe the pitch of the roof seems to be a crucial symbolic element in the perception of "home."[7]

The apparent universality of the image of homes as freestanding dwelling units, at least among Western European cultures, would suggest that an acultural approach to design is possible. This was, in fact, one of the underlying premises of the "international style," which assumed that most life-styles can adapt to Western building forms and that the understanding and acceptance of building forms will be similar across cultures (or should be!). In a comparison of the preferences of architecture students in Scotland

and Australia for different types of house forms, some of which were the most prevalent types in each culture (row houses in Glasgow and single-family houses in Australia), Canter and Thorne found that the architecture students did not prefer the most prevalent building type in their area.[8] Rather, they preferred a building type that did not represent the mainstream. In Australia these were old row houses with ornate iron grillwork, which had become a status symbol among the intellectuals and avant-garde, and in Glasgow these were suburban single-family houses. Given architectural education's emphasis on the unique and special case, it does not seem surprising, in retrospect, that both groups preferred what was statistically an unusual type of residence in their situation.

The findings appear to be a function of the groups selected to participate in the study. If the same study had been performed using lower-, middle-, and working-class persons, it is likely that for these groups, who are more uncertain about their social status and generally aspire to be *like* others, that the Australians would prefer the detached cottage and the Scottish the row house (although if they thought it were attainable, I suspect the Scottish would also prefer detached cottages). These findings do not support the assumption about a universal image of home, but they do suggest that images vary as a function of social class and educational background and that within social groups there is a desire for a home that is in some way unique, or individually or group identifiable, and that in some way raises the self-esteem of the occupants and reflects their values.

In trying to understand low-income people's image of "home," it is important to realize that a type of hierarchical principle operates where the most basic need, in a biological sense, is for house as shelter, a place that provides protection from potentially damaging or unpleasant trauma or other events.[9] It is primarily for the middle class, where it is accepted as a given that the home is a *safe* place, that more attention is paid to the house as a means for self-expression and self-realization. People concerned about the cold, plumbing, and rats do not have the luxury of worrying about the image of their home; as these concerns are alleviated, more and more attention is paid to image.[10] It is among the middle class, in particular, that the house as image of self surfaces.

In a study of how suburbanites chose their homes Carl Werthman found that extroverted, self-made businessmen tended to choose somewhat ostentatious, mock-colonial homes, while people in the helping professions, whose goals revolved around personal satisfaction rather than financial success, tended to opt for the quieter, unique architect-designed houses conforming to current standards of "good taste."[11] For these middle-income groups, the house is an effective way to reflect personal values and their image of self. It is different in form from the hand-built houses described earlier but similar in purpose.

Architects and planners sometimes argue that people have been conditioned to want a freestanding house-on-the-ground through advertising, model-home salesmen, and the images portrayed on television. Clare Cooper-Marcus feels these media reflect only what appears to be a universal need for a house form in which the "self and family unit can be seen as separate, unique, private, and protected." Cooper-Marcus continues:

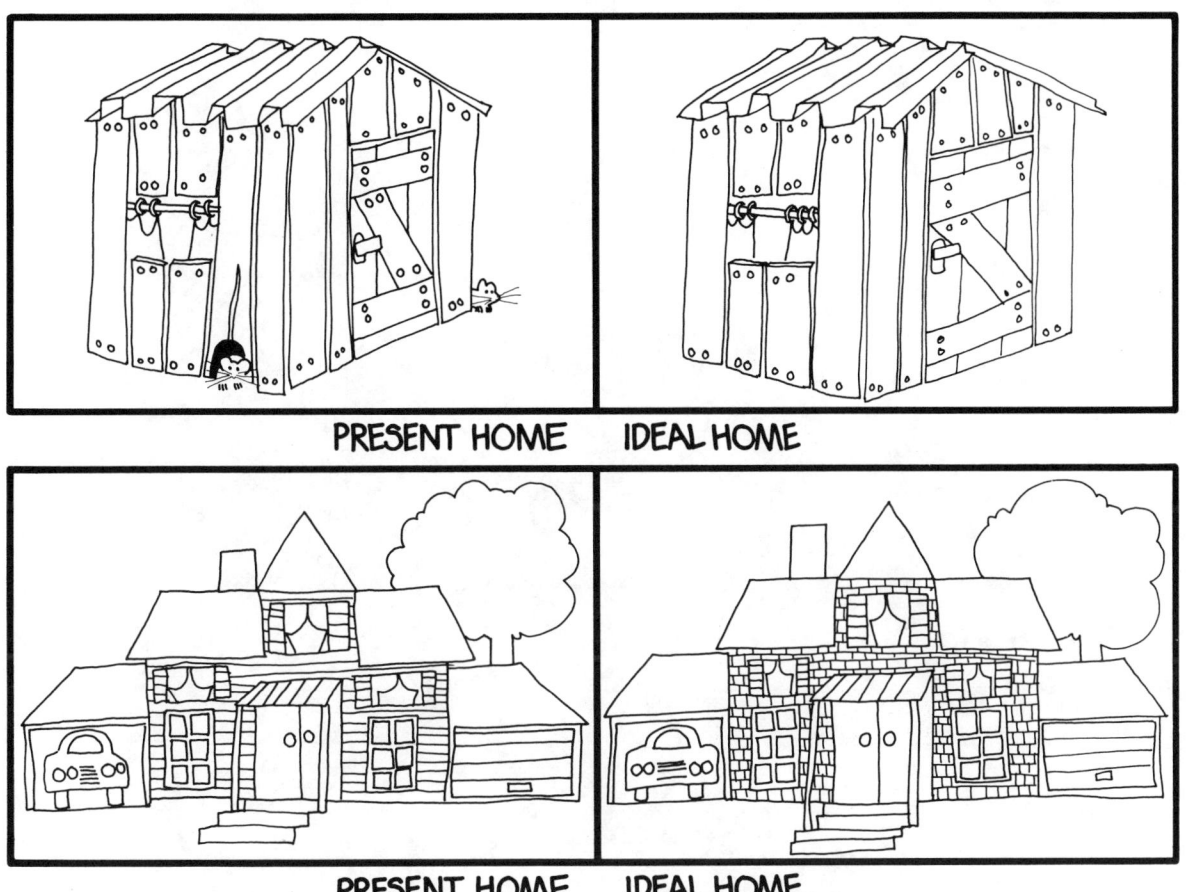

PRESENT HOME   IDEAL HOME

PRESENT HOME   IDEAL HOME

The high-rise apartment building is rejected by most Americans as a family home because, I would suggest, it gives one no territory on the ground, violates the archaic image of what a house is, and is perceived unconsciously as a threat to one's self-image as a separate and unique personality. The house form in which people are being asked to live is not a symbol-of-self, but the symbol of a stereotyped, anonymous filing-cabinet collection of selves, which people fear they are becoming.[12]

Her thesis is supported, in part, by Michelson's data, cited earlier, which showed that providing the economic benefits of a single-family owned house in multifamily houses (condominiums) was not seen as a satisfactory substitute for owning a single-family home.[13] Cooper-Marcus also argues that providing some of the features of a house, as well as opportunities for modification and ownership, will still not satisfy the majority of lower- and middle-income American families' image of permanent house.

My own research on low- and moderate-

20 *Housing Messages*

Figure 2-1
The *ideal* house is a single-family dwelling with pitched roof, wood siding, and separated from surrounding houses by a large and well-landscaped lot.

Figure 2-2
This house is not as desirable as the *ideal* house because it has less landscaping and land around it, but it is still quite desirable since it is a single-family, detached house with a pitched roof.

income multifamily housing was predicated on the assumption that although no multifamily housing may be a completely satisfactory substitute for a single-family house, it was likely that different types of multifamily housing were still able to reflect one's self-image or desired status and self-esteem to a different degree, based in part on their physical characteristics.[14] The assumption was that the more "features" multifamily housing design included that were similar to those found in single-family detached houses, the more satisfactory the multifamily housing would be.

Figure 2-3
The mobile home may not be a *real* house, but it is for a single family, it is detached, and it can be afforded by low-income families. No apartment complex has all of these features.

Most architects consider aesthetics and formalistic design qualities to be central in the creation of a positive image and appearance. A study of seven low- and high-rise developments for low- and moderate-income residents sponsored by the New York State Urban Development Corporation (UDC) found four major factors contributed to residents' evaluation of the appearance of their development: (1) maintenance, (2) landscaping, (3) outside materials, and (4) shape and layout of buildings.[15]

For many residents appearance was closely tied to good upkeep. Well-maintained grounds and the absence of litter and junk were a prerequisite to satisfaction with any more specific design feature. As maintenance problems decreased, residents became more aware of other aspects of the development's appearance and the "public face" it presented.

Lobbies in high-rise buildings, for instance, were areas of concern because they conveyed in a single glance a picture of wealth, habitation, neglect, or respectability. It is through these semipublic spaces that friends, relatives, and visitors pass on their way to visit residents. As one resident put it after noting that the lobby needed draperies, plants, and paintings, it looked "naked." Residents wanted their visitors and themselves to feel like they had walked into a home, not an office or institution.

Landscaping, including well-maintained grass, trees, and shrubs, contributed significantly to overall satisfaction, whether it resulted from a naturally wooded area surrounding the development or from planned landscaping that compensated for rectilinear building forms, which, as one resident put it, looked "like barracks."

Outside materials at the low-rise developments ranged from unfinished wood to stained wood and brick mixtures. Some residents considered naturally weathered wood attractive, but for others it was taken as a sign of poor maintenance and contributed to the feeling that over time the development would slowly deteriorate. For this group of persons, unfinished wood had the image of being somewhat flimsy and unsturdy, particularly in comparison to brick. The one site that combined brick and stained wood was liked tremendously, primarily because the combination of materials conveyed an image of sturdiness and quality that unfinished wood or brick alone could not provide.

Residents preferred some type of peaked roof, as well as the absence of geometric order in the layout of the buildings because both provide visual variety and are associated more with residential than industrial and commercial buildings.

In a more systematic attempt to understand the nature of perceived diversity in building form, Pyron found that judgments of diversity of building layout increased linearly with a reduction of redundancy in the layout (the same patterns do not repeat themselves again and again), although he found that the diversity of the building *forms* themselves were more important in judgments of diversity than the manner in which they were laid out.[16] This finding is not surprising if building and site form are considered from the perspective of a person living in a particular part of a site, as opposed to having a bird's-eye view of it. What can be seen from any given point in the development is primarily the form of the individual dwelling units. One of the architect's major problems is that by relying on two-dimensional plans, he or she tends to look at overall patterns as though the whole place can be viewed at once, neglecting the fact that some buildings block others in reality and what one actually can see at any given point in time and space is limited.[17]

The fact that 67 percent of the UDC residents, on the average, felt that the outside appearance of their development was "very important" seems to support architects' concern and emphasis on the aesthetic character of buildings. The residents' concern was not for form itself, however, but for form as it affected their social standing in the community, as well as their own satisfaction. Outside appearance was important because it reflected one's "own reputation" and "if it doesn't look good, we won't like it." As one resident said, "If you bring a friend here, it has to be nice on the outside; it looks more like a home, not just a building."

In an attempt to get a more in-depth view of the physical referents people used to evaluate the appearance of multifamily housing and to learn more about what made multifamily housing more or less "home-like," Lawrence Friedberg did a small exploratory substudy using two of the UDC developments.[18] His small and selected sample makes the results tentative, but they are strengthened by their congruence with the UDC data and other research.

Eighteen UDC residents living in town house units (more than one living level in each apartment) were randomly selected from two low-rise developments and asked to rate twelve photographs along a like-dislike dimension and then to indicate what it was about these places that influenced their judgments. The twelve photographs were of low-rise multifamily housing developments that varied in form, landscaping, and materials. No attempt was made to control each variable systematically. The interview technique used was "successive probing"; only a few basic questions were asked each respondent, but for each of these broad, open-ended questions, the interviewer continued to probe each response until the respondent was unable to add anything else. All interviews were tape-recorded.

Using seven categories developed on the basis of the data collected, Friedberg found the developments that received the highest overall ratings had the following characteristics: (for function) private entry, balconies, exterior lighting, the relationship of parking to the dwelling units, and play areas; (for shape, pattern, and form) "breaks in line" and variation in shapes; (for landscaping) lawns, trees, bushes, and so on; (for general visual appearance) respondents said these developments were beautiful, looked like a house, and were modern or not modern (both positive).

If one category (for example, landscaping), received a very high score, this could compensate for a lower score on another category (for example, shape, pattern, and form). However, function, shape, pattern, and form, and landscaping were the most powerful dimensions. Scoring low on one of these, but high on another category (say, construction materials/color) would *not* substantially increase the overall rating of the development. Those developments that received the lowest overall evaluation presented a mirror image of the highest-rated developments. Almost all of the comments about these developments were negative. Residents disliked shared entrances, apartments stacked on top of each other, the absence of play areas and landscaping, and flat and straight forms forming "one big cinder block."

An important finding for architects was that residents could appreciate what architects designed, but this appreciation was contingent upon the design's maximizing the expression of individual place, residence, and territory. Forms that identified individual dwelling units through setbacks and private porches and patios do this very well. Extensive landscaping was able to mask the lack of individuality in undistinguished blocks of units. Designs that maximized the expression of individual territory were preferred more than those that did not, apparently because individual territory was associated with residents' image of a freestanding house. These design considerations were appreciated, but the second part of Friedberg's study suggested they did not substitute for the "real" thing—a single-family detached house.

In the second part of his study, Friedberg asked residents directly what contributed to their images of "home." In response to essentially one question "What is a home?" he was able to loosely group residents' responses into six categories: (1) privacy; (2) play facilities; (3) restrictions on life-style; (4) control; (5) personalization and adaptation; and (6) storage.

Privacy Several levels of privacy surfaced in the interviews, among them privacy from neighbors, privacy among family members, visual privacy, and acoustical privacy, each required in different amounts for different respondents. Privacy from neighbors centered mostly upon outside characteristics of the unit and visual access from the outside to the inside. Privacy among family members was most often related to physical separation and a feeling of personal isolation. In response

26   *Housing Messages*

Figure 2-4
Desired visual complexity can be achieved through manipulation of design elements.

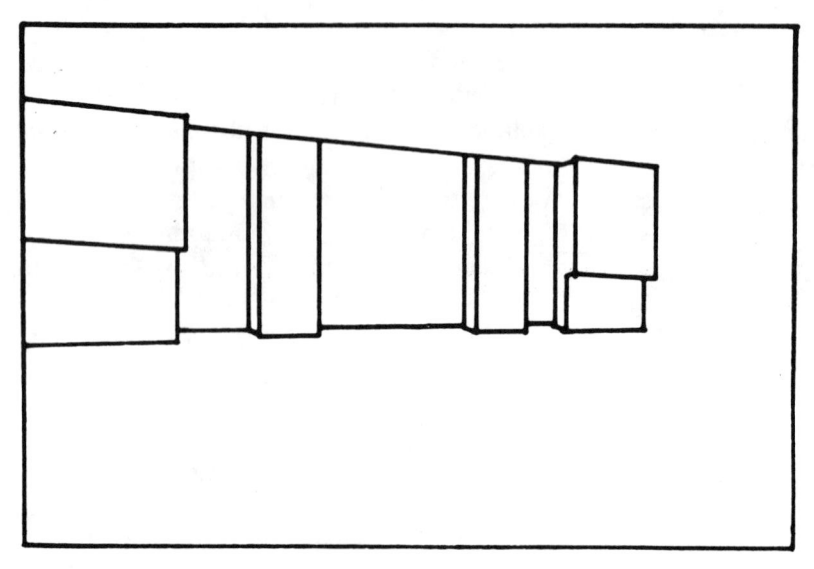

A relatively simple building form

placed in complex context—rated highly.

Courtesy of Lawrence P. Friedberg

to the question, "How does the arrangement of this apartment satisfy your needs?" one resident said:

> As far as I'm concerned this is ideal for me. See, when I first came here, they wanted to give me all on one floor. I didn't want that because I can't get away from my kids, and my kids [sixteen-year-old twin boys] can't get away from me when we're all together on one floor. And my children study music and practice a lot, so if I sent them to the other room, I can still hear them, where if they go upstairs and close the door, I can hear them, but not so much as if they were on the same floor.

Another resident discussed the psychological separation provided by multifloor units:

> ... the interior design of the split level where you have privacy from other members of the family too, because like the children could be playing in the top level in their room whereas you'll be entertaining downstairs and the noise wouldn't *seem* so much around each other ... like if all these rooms were on one floor, one level, they are small, you know the rooms aren't that big, but because they are spread out with the seven stairs in between each floor, it makes it *seem* like a larger apartment than it really is.

The separation or ability to separate activities is related to the psychological size of the apartment. This appeared to be one of the outstanding characteristics of a "home" to many persons:

> I think it's quite like a home, the fact that it's multi-level. You're not all on one floor, that you have room to move, space to differentiate activities in ... you have a sense, even though the kitchen is attached to the dining area, that there is a spatial separation ... you have a living room that's separated, that you can actually go into, you know, it's like there, makes it much easier to keep clean. You have more sense of privacy for different individuals, you don't feel like you're on top of one another all the time, you can go to a different floor in a different place and noise doesn't carry as much and ... even though it's a very small space, they've utilized it well.

This respondent had recently moved from a single-family detached house into a four-bedroom duplex unit. The family was comprised of five persons.

The duplex town house type unit provided a high degree of privacy according to several respondents:

> I think that the way that the buildings are arranged and the way the apartments are arranged are more like a home than any other type apartment complex just because of the design. The singly attached townhouse style living is unlike an apartment in a typical sample because there is no one living over you and no one living under you and what privacy there can be is maximum privacy I guess for apartment living.

Again, in terms of "homelike" features, another respondent, who also lived in a duplex town-house type apartment, further qualified the meaning.

> ... most of it (not being like a home) is on the outside where it doesn't seem like our own home [This comment followed a discussion about the problems encountered with children playing outside], but on the inside it does. ...

Interviewer: Why does it seem so on the inside?

Respondent: I guess just because of the way it's built.... It's kind of like a house in itself even though there are other people on the other side.

Interviewer: What is it about the way that it's built that makes it like a house?

Respondent: I don't know, I guess it's just because nobody is over you or on top of you. You come and go as you please.

Some of the psychological consequences of a lack of acoustical privacy were quite clearly illustrated in the comments of one resident.

...you are much closer to your neighbors, you really are...and unfortunately the sound does carry through the walls, you hear them run their water in the sink, ah...flush the toilet, take a shower, move the furniture, even conversation in a loud tone...it's bad to hear other people's fights to know that your own can be heard.

The absence of exterior privacy was frequently noted and seemed to stem in part from unclearly defined exterior territory.

There is no privacy in the yard. You know, you don't have a separate enclosed area to call your own. Yeah, that's one thing that really bugs me. I'm a privacy bug.

Some residents viewed the amount of exterior privacy differently.

...you can go sit out here, it's *like* a little porch out here and also in the back there is grass back there, you can go out and sit back there and you know, get a suntan.

The desire for outside privacy and territorial definition for many persons is quite strong for both practical and psychological reasons.

...and like what this girl has out there, that fence [a fence installed by a resident], she can't have that out there, they [the management] told her she could build it and after she built it they told her she would have to take it out and she paid too much money for it to take it out so...you can't have any fence here, you can't have anything that, you know, like a permanent thing out there, like you could when you have your own home.

External privacy, which provides some separation among neighbors, is an important component of user satisfaction. One respondent gave a clear description of the relationships she felt appropriate with neighbors.

...I go out in the day. I work. My sons are in school for the day so nobody is home. We're only home when they come in about four, and I come in at four-thirty, five o'clock, and the only contact I have with most of the people is from five o'clock on, and in winter you don't see anybody and in the summer you see them for a short while.

Interviewer: Do you prefer not to have to deal with other people?

Respondent: No, I like people, but I don't butt into other people's business, and I don't expect them to do that to me. I'm very friendly. If they come in and say "can I borrow this?" "Can I borrow that?" Why not? Cause I might run out instead of, traveling or walking all the way to the store it's a lot easier to go next door and say, Hey! can you loan me a cup of sugar, or whatever.

A large proportion of the respondents have this same attitude. In terms of site design and the encouragement of relations among neighbors, the implication seems to relate back to the control of social interactions. "I like people, but I don't butt into other people's business and I don't expect them to do that to me." Friendships can be on many levels in multifamily housing, but the ability to control that level of friendship or provide for privacy seems to be primary to the respondents in this study.

> ... you have privacy, of course your neighbors are right there, but I don't bother with the neighbors anyway. I mind my own business, and I expect them to do the same.

> I guess I kind of value my privacy. If I want to do things without the neighbors watching me every minute, I would be able to do it if I had my own home.

> [*Interviewer:* What makes it a house?]

> I don't know. I guess it's just because nobody is over you or on top of you. You come and go as you please. Of course the neighbors are nosey [laugh], but that's to be expected.

Comments of a respondent living in a single-level garden apartment further illuminated some of the homelike qualities of the duplex town house and how locational features of a garden apartment contributed to a feeling of "home."

> Well, I'm glad I'm on the end, and I'm glad I'm on the ground floor....

> *Interviewer:* What is it about the end and ground floor location that you like?

> *Respondent:* It's more ... it doesn't seem like an apartment because you're not tracking through a hall where everybody is, you're on an end ... you don't have people right smack next to you on either side.

> *Interviewer:* You don't track through a hall, what do you mean?

> *Respondent:* I mean like all the upstairs apartments you've got three doors in the one hall. Where here, I just have to come out off the sidewalk into my own apartment, and I'm the only one coming to my door.

Vertical separation of units so that there were no upstairs or downstairs neighbors provided one of the most potent homelike features in these multifamily schemes. The privacy and control provided by a private entry was very important to the feelings of freedom expressed by the respondents, the freedom to "come and go as you please."

In the UDC study most residents felt an outside private entrance was "very important," and it was much more important for families with children than families without them. For families with children, a private entrance meant that their children were going through public spaces less often and therefore needed to be controlled less in their relationship to other residents. Private entrances should also increase the satisfaction of families without children because of the decreased noise and activity that is generated by childrens' coming and going through public corridors, elevators, and stairwells.

Respondents in the UDC study saw privacy in terms of the "ability to control unwanted social interactions," and there was a significant correlation between resident satisfaction with privacy and general satisfaction. In combination with a significant correlation between the feeling of being "at home" and general satisfaction, these data suggest that being able to control access into and activities within the dwelling unit is a major factor in residents' overall satisfaction with living in the development. The general uproar that often follows management's making "inspections" and other unsolicited calls in apartments seems largely due to the great importance residents attach to being able to control access to their individual dwelling units.

Most residents did not relate privacy to noise. Families without children were the most dissatisfied. UDC residents were particularly disturbed by "intimate" noises, such as hearing neighbors' conversations at normal volume, toilets flushing, and people sneezing. They were able to tolerate noises normally associated with apartment living, such as hearing neighbors' children playing or music through the walls, but poor soundproofing was a source of tension, particularly for parents who were concerned about their children's play bothering neighbors. They tried to keep noise levels down, but they were unhappy and unsuccessful trying to control behaviors that would not be a problem in a single-family house.

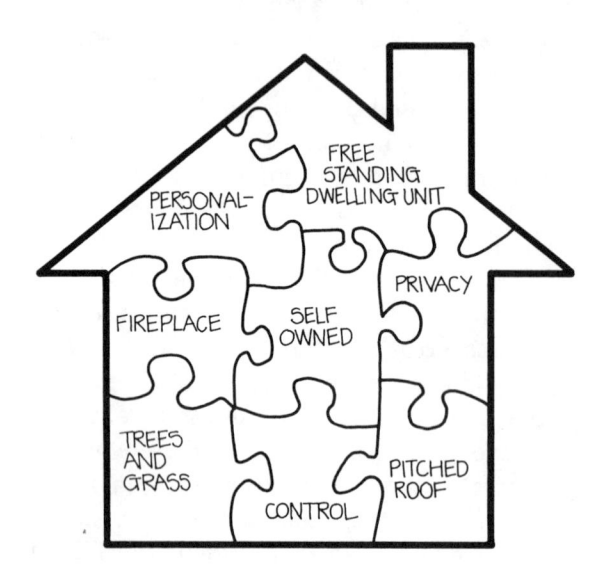

Play facilities Most single-family houses incorporate backyards suited for small children's play, and most images of "home" include some parklike qualities ideal for play. The provision of adequate play facilities for all ages of children is a vital consideration in development of satisfactory multifamily environments. Play space or its absence affects both those with and without children.

Interviewer: What are some of the things that make this different from a home?

Respondent: ... yard space mainly, you are close to neighbors, you're, you know, it's very close. It's not as bad as other type apartments but it's not as good as a home ... because the yard space is small, the traffic in front of your apartment, all the children playing around.

Outdoor private or semiprivate space can act as a buffer between dwelling units and separate the inevitable activity of children from those who are bothered by it. The particular location of playgrounds in relation to groups of units they are intended to serve is also critical:

They have playgrounds all around here, and in this section our playground is right down there. They refused to allow the kids in this area to go down there on account of the Day Care Center ... they have the playground up to 4 P.M. so therefore our kids go out there and get in trouble.

They get in the mall and start digging up that mall, and we get hell about that. You can't keep an eye on them all the time, and for me to send them away the hell over there by the playground, I wouldn't do that... they told me we would be able to look out of the kitchen windows [and supervise the children].

The difficulties caused by inadequate or poorly placed play facilities are widespread. Children inevitably cause "damage" to the site, and the parents are reprimanded by the management. If the needs of the children are understood and provided for and the requirements of the parents for supervision of the children are known and designed for, the potential conflict and dissatisfactions encountered can be minimized. Part of the problem is clearly related to social and life-style differences and ages of children. The conflicts are not only among the parents, children, and management but also among the children of different ages.

(This respondent was moving to a trailer on her own land and in response to the question of how will it be different the reply was:) I won't have to worry so much as I do here about other kids walking up and punching them in the nose. If they were older it would be better here you know... with them being so small (4 years, 21 months, and 9 months) it's hard to try and clean house and be outside at the same time watching the kids so whenever they go outside I have to go outside, except for my oldest, and I can let him go out and just keep an eye on him.

Another resident gave an additional dimension to the problem of different-aged children and their requirements for play.

... now the playgrounds they have set up here are mainly up to 5 year olds, my children are past that age (7, 11, and 18 year old sons)... now I'd like to see a little field for the 8 to 12 and then the 12 through the teenagers, so they would have a place to play then they wouldn't get into trouble.

Another resident expressed quite clearly some of the dilemmas parents face in solving the play problem for children.

... I guess there is so many kids and so little open area and like we can't set up a swing set all the kids have got to use it and now I have four, three little ones and they're just toddlers and it's hard because like the big swing sets is down across the road and the way the cars and trucks go through, I just can't let him go and I don't know, I have to restrict them so much. Well, I guess if I had my own home, I would build a fence around it because of them being so small and put them in it.

Restrictions on life-style In terms of limiting the homelike qualities of the developments studied, restrictions to life-style were relatively low priority to those interviewed.

Well, you are restricted to do certain things.

Interviewer: What sort of things?

Respondent: We... like the children are not allowed, well I can see if they just run on the grass, they forget... they have somebody working here on the grounds telling them you're not supposed to do this and you're not supposed to do that. I as a parent can tell them what to do, you know, I know right from wrong. You know what I mean.

This respondent's concern is not so much that her children are restricted but that she is not the one who determines what the restrictions will be. The fact that it is someone else who determines "right from wrong" was seen as restricting her role as a parent. The setting of rules by someone else would *not* occur in a *real* home where the occupant *is* the manager. The establishment of rules as a joint effort of management and residents is one way to solve the need for rules without creating the feeling of having one's role and authority as parent undermined by someone outside the family who is perceived as imposing arbitrary rules. The same anger and frustration of having someone else impose restrictions on one's life-style was noted by a resident who said:

> No, they're (the management) decent as far as the rules. The office called, two, three times saying we had a lot of company. It's nobody's business how much company you have. I mean whether it was true or it wasn't, as long as you're not rowdy or noisy or disturbing the peace, I don't see where this is right. It's not like having a home of your own where you could come and go and do as you please.

These quotes suggest that much of the desire for a "house" is based not on architectural features but on the freedom to structure one's activities as one pleases without undue interference. Yet living in close proximity to neighbors—especially when facilities must be shared—makes involvement with neighbors almost inevitable. Most residents realize that living in close proximity requires rules of some sort:

> We do just about anything we want here, really. You can have people over, as long as the noise isn't too much. You can have a party or have company or people over for the weekend. Of course, you have to keep it down because there are people next door.

In the UDC study there were few perceived restrictions on activities within the dwelling unit, but many of these also involved conflicts among people, especially children and their parents. Three different strategies for coping with these conflicts became apparent: (1) *time territory,* in which people used different rooms for different purposes at different times; (2) *space territory,* in which persons wishing to engage in different activities would go to different rooms; and (3) *cooperation-capitulation,* in which case everyone does the one activity determined by the dominant group (for example, everyone watching television, or turning off the television and everyone being quiet).

Arrangement of space in which incompatible activities can be separated by different floor levels, for instance, is one way of solving activity problems in small spaces. The UDC data indicated, however, that the kinds of activities restricted in single level and town-house type units were similar. Size per se appeared to be more important than any particular interior room arrangement, although these data may be a consequence of none of the arrangements' effectively utilizing minimum space standards.

The restricted amount of space created a dilemma for parents. They found that they either had to restrict their children's "messy" activities (which produce dirt, clutter, or take a long time to complete) or abandon some of their own standards of cleanliness.

Maintaining a "respectable" household was in many cases intricately bound with one's own self-esteem.

Residents' concept of the appropriate location for different activities may inhibit their looking for alternative ways of coping with space limitations. Stevenson et al., in their study *High Living,* gave the example of a mother who restricted her son's model building because the only space available was his bed, and she did not like dirt and glue getting on the bedspread. She made no attempt to provide a protective cover, apparently because she considered such activities simply inappropriate for inside the house.[19] The barrier here is a psychological, or even a cultural, one. Education about creative alternatives may help, but knowing the kinds of associations people have between activities and their location in (or out of) the home and using this information as a basis for design is likely to be more successful.

Given a choice, most UDC residents preferred special-purpose rooms: a dining room to eat in, a playroom to play in, a laundry room to wash in. A separate dining area, for example, could also accommodate formal dining room furniture. Being unable to display culturally appropriate furniture was a source of frustration and embarrassment for some residents.

It was *not* the case that people most preferred the arrangement they had. Many residents had lived in single- or two-family dwellings prior to moving to the UDC development, and their prior experiences with separate dining rooms or other arrangements provided them with images of "home" at odds with the arrangement available in their new multifamily housing. Future generations may grow up believing a combined living-dining room is an acceptable arrangement and eat-in kitchens are a part of history, but for the foreseeable future, special-purpose rooms are likely to be seen as a characteristic of a "real" house.

Control The desire to control one's environment extended beyond the issue of and the desire to control unwanted social interaction. It embraced the desire to make decisions that reflect individual lifestyles, tastes, and even bodily comfort. Mundane decisions like setting a thermostat are taken for granted by most people in single-family homes, yet a single thermostat for an entire building controlled by the "Super" is a constant reminder to residents that they are not in control over even the most mundane decisions, but are considered an average mass of humanity.

> ...well, you know, general things like you have your own washer/dryer hook-up if you have a washer and dryer. In a lot of apartment complexes you have one wash room that everyone uses all the time...and things like, you know, individual water heater and individual furnace it's not, *you can control it yourself; it's not controlled by maintenance staff or management.*

Not all residents wanted the responsibility of control. There are advantages to renting rather than owning a home:

> One thing that scares me about owning a home would be paying the utilities which would vary every month, whereas when you pay your rent, you pay one sum and it includes everything, and I like the feature of apartment living. And no taxes, you know, things like that.

Personalization and adaptation Several respondents differentiated between having one's own home and apartment living in terms of what changes or modifications they could make:

> ...for the most part it's pretty much like having your own home, really, except you know, you don't paint the walls or anything but ah, you know, in my own home I'd like to have the walls a different color.... Of course, that might run into money but it would break the monotony. ...As it is you walk into your neighbor's apartment, and it looks essentially just like yours does because it's the same color and everything.

One respondent had a clear-cut idea of how to personalize her apartment:

> Well, I'd fix up the outside, I'd do landscaping, that's the first thing I'd do...I'd put a little more personality outside. It doesn't have any personality, really, you know, when you walk up.

Another person said:

> I would also like to see some kind of facility for linens...the bathroom has only a medicine chest which is lovely, except that people do have blankets, sheets, towels, and assorted paraphernalia that should be stored someplace, and it could very easily have been accommodated in the design upstairs, there's plenty room for one, obviously we can't build our own.

In the UDC study 70 percent of the residents wanted to select the color of the dwelling unit interior, for two reasons: to allow for individual expression and to increase the utility and convenience of the apartment. One resident summed up both reasons:

> ...every floor has this tile, this color and it's monotonous, they could have thought of something better, something more practical, especially for a kitchen and dining room than a white floor and white walls, something that's easier to keep clean. When you move into a brand new place you really want to keep it clean, and you're frustrated by the fact that it's an endless battle, forever.

Storage Storage proved to be a problem for a good proportion of the respondents interviewed. The lack of storage for infrequently used and large items was a particular problem. In response to the question, "How would your ideal home be different from this?" one person said:

> We would have more room. More storage space.

Interviewer: What kind of storage space?

Respondent: Well, like in my living room I've got the "Porta-crib," the baby's "Swing-o-matic" and there's hardly any room for us to move around in the living room and up in the bedroom is the same thing because with them being so little, you have to have so many things.... When they're older, they don't have to have.... Like I would have a separate play room for them if I had my own home, and like I left some toys at my mother-in-law's where if I had my own home, I would be able to have them here.

Another resident spoke of a different aspect of the lack of storage space.

> ...as far as storage goes, we don't have any.

Interviewer: What kinds of things can't you store?

Respondent: Oh, like your grills, your children's strollers, their playpens when they outgrow them, you know, that kind of thing, your winter clothes ... old books from my husband's school, he doesn't want to throw that money away ... just stuff people put in their attic.

These responses suggest that at least a part of what makes a house more desirable than apartment living is functional considerations—almost any house has more storage space than an apartment has. Images of homes appear to have as an important component the *expectation* of great functionality, as well as control and individuality.

SUMMARY

Our data and others' research suggest that it is unlikely that multifamily housing, regardless of its design, will be as satisfying for most Americans as living in a detached single-family house. But for those persons who are forced to live in multifamily housing, design features that increase both internal and external privacy and that make dwelling units individually identifiable, even if the means is similar for each apartment, can at least make multifamily housing a little more homelike. Pitched roofs and materials such as brick and finished wood (at least on the East Coast) also seem to represent the image of a sturdy and substantial house in contrast to unfinished wood and flat roofs. Chapter 4, "Personalization," will discuss how the provision for external privacy in the form of well-defined porches and balconies facilitates the individual modification of essentially identical units and in some ways approximates the "variations on a model" that characterizes most vernacular architecture. In some very simple but basic ways, the freedom to modify and personalize one's exterior and interior spaces symbolizes the freedom to control one's own activities and reflect one's own life-style, and these are elements closely associated with images of "home."

REFERENCES

1. R. Cramer, "Images of Home," *AIA Journal* 46 (1960): 41-49.
2. W. Michelson, "Most People Don't Want What Architects Want," *Trans-Action* (July-August 1968): 37-43.

3. W. Mangin, "Urbanization Case History in Peru," *Architectural Design* 33 (1963): 369, cited by A. Rapoport, *House Form and Culture* (Englewood Cliffs, N.J.: Prentice-Hall, 1969).
4. J. Fitchen, "An Anthropological Perspective on Poverty and Antipoverty Programs," *Human Ecology Forum* 5 (1975): 222-224. See also J. Fitchen, "Rural Slum Housing in the Northeastern U.S.: An Anthropological Study of Causes and Cures" (unpublished manuscript, March 1976).
5. J. B. Jackson, "The Westward Moving House: Three American Houses and the People Who Live in Them," *Landscape* 2 (1953): 8-21.
6. Ibid.
7. Rapoport, *House Form and Culture*.
8. D. Canter, and R. Thorne. "Attitudes to Housing: A Cross Cultural Comparison," *Environment and Behavior* 4 (1972): 1.
9. L. Rainwater, "Fear and House-as-Haven in the Lower Class," *Journal of American Institute of Planners* 32 (1966): 23-37.
10. F. D. Becker, *Design for Living: The Residents' View of Multifamily Housing* (Ithaca, N.Y.: Center for Urban Development Research, Cornell University, 1974).
11. C. Werthman, "The Social Meaning of the Physical Environment" (Ph.D. diss., University of California, Berkeley, 1968), cited by C. Cooper, "The House as Symbol of Self," in J. Lang et al., eds., *Architecture and Human Behavior*. (Stroudsburg, Pa.: Dowden, Hutchinson & Ross, 1974).
12. C. Cooper, "The House as Symbol of Self," in J. Lang et al. (eds.) *Architecture and Human Behavior* (Stroudsburg, Pa.: Dowden, Hutchinson & Ross, 1974).
13. Michelson, "Most People."
14. Becker, *Design for Living*.
15. Ibid.
16. B. Pyron, "Form and Space in Human Habitat: Judgmental and Attitude Responses," *Environment and Behavior* 4 (1972): 87-120.
17. J. Lang, "Theories of Perception and 'Formal' Design," in J. Lang et al. (eds.) *Designing for Human Behavior: Architecture and the Behavior of Sciences* (Stroudsburg, Pa.: Dowden, Hutchinson & Ross, 1974).
18. L. Friedberg, "Comparative Perceptions of Residential Environment and 'Home' Image, Verbal Responses and Physical Reference" (Master's thesis, Cornell University, 1974).
19. A. Stevenson, E. Martin, and J. O'Neil, *High Living: A Study of Family Life in Flats* (New York: Cambridge University Press, 1967).

3
Public Housing

Given the importance of symbolic aspects of housing for the users' self-esteem and image, why has public housing developed the image it has? Ask your neighbor to describe public housing, and you will probably get a description of dilapidated, monotonous, multifamily housing, with flat roofs and minimal landscaping and inhabited primarily by large black families on welfare. This image of public housing, only partially correct, is tied to misconceptions about what public housing *is* and the social context out of which it evolved.

To some the term *public housing* implies dwellings that are owned by a federal, state, or local government or public body. To others, it signifies that dwellings are financed by a government, government body, or government agency. Under either of these definitions, public housing has been part of our governmental program from the country's inception, since the government has always provided barracks and quarters for troops and their families on military posts. The Department of Defense held title to more than 70,000 family housing units at the end of 1958.[1]

Public housing is far from exclusively public in terms of its development and construction. Dwellings are often designed by private architects and built by private contractors; local real estate persons are paid for appraising and acquiring the land; supplies and materials are bought from private businessmen; the construction workers are not government employees; and most families are private rather than public employees.

The federal government's involvement with public housing is generally considered to have begun with the Housing Act of 1937, and its history and the role of government and private business in framing this and subsequent housing laws, as well as the housing codes that preceded them, are crucial in understanding the physical form public housing has taken in this country and its consequent social stigma.

In a trenchant analysis of public housing, Friedman described two alternative rationalizations used for initial public-housing legislation as well as subsequent laws.[2] One is what he called the "social-cost" approach, in which problems with slums and inadequate housing are analyzed in terms of the costs imposed by the slums on society at large. The second rationalization he called the "welfare" approach: it views inadequate housing in terms of the cost the slums impose on the people who live in them. Social legislation is proposed and defended on one or both of these bases: either it helps the poor or some worthy class, or by helping the poor it helps us all.

The Housing Act of 1937 was predicated primarily on the social-cost approach and the idea that substandard housing represented a hazard to public welfare because it fostered social disorders heightened by the danger of fire or collapse. This landmark legislation also suggested that slum conditions were inimical to the general welfare of the nation by: encouraging the spread of disease and lowering the level of health, morale, and vitality of large portions of the American people; increasing the hazards of fire, accidents, and natural calamities; subjecting the moral standards of the young to bad influences; increasing the violation of the criminal laws; impairing industrial and agricultural productive efficiencies; lowering the standards of living of large groups of Americans; necessitating the vast and extraordinary expenditure of public funds . . . for crime prevention, punishment and correction, fire prevention, public health service, and relief.[3]

The same social-cost approach was reflected in the more florid writing of Jacob Riis's famous exposé *How the Other Half Lives* almost fifty years earlier, in 1890, when he wrote that slums were "the hot-beds of epidemics that carry death to rich and poor alike; the nurseries of pauperism and crime [which bred a] scum of 40,000 human wrecks in the insane asylums and work houses year by year." The tenements "turned out in the last 8 years around half a million beggars to prey upon our charities," and they "maintained a standing army of 10,000 tramps." Above all, Riis wrote that the tenements touched family life with a "deadly moral contagion."[4]

The belief that the kind of problems that plagued slums affected those living around them was a major reason for earlier reform legislation. Most of the initial housing legislation was noncontroversial because it concentrated on the physical dangers associated with slums and how these could affect nearby middle-class housing. In New York, for example, pre-Revolutionary laws tried to prevent people from keeping hay, straw, pitch, tar, and turpentine where the danger of fire was great, and a 1766 law created a fire zone where houses had to be made of stone or brick with slate or tile roofs.[5] The New York Tenement House Law of 1867 was different because it applied only to dwellings, particularly "tenements," that were defined as houses or buildings (or portions thereof) that were rented, leased, let, or hired out to be occupied as the home or residence of more than three families living independently of one another.[6] This definition covered all the houses in the slum areas and virtually none of the houses of the wealthy. Friedman feels that this law was the evolutionary root of all succeeding housing and tenement codes. It ordered tenement and lodging houses to be equipped with ventilators, fire escapes, water closets, garbage receptacles, adequate chimneys, and so forth. Essentially this law, like others, assumed that a slum was a physical entity and that control of physical abuses per se could solve its evils. Unfortunately, the 1867 law was adopted by few states or municipalities, and even where it was adopted, it was poorly enforced.

Friedman attributes the successful enactment of tenement-house reform to several factors: (1) a heightened perception of the problem of urban slums; (2) a corps of dedicated and organized reform workers committed to housing reform; (3) the absence of strong ideological opposition; (4) the absence of strong economic opposition. In contrast to the direct involvement of federal and state government in the design, construction, and management of housing units, tenement laws were not considered socialistic since they required no direct government intervention, only "regulations," and they were therefore considered "moderate" in scope. In contrast to the tremendous influence exerted by the National Association of Real Estate Boards on the form of subsequent public-housing legislation and building, the early tenement laws were opposed primarily by slum landlords who lived in the slums themselves or who were relatively recent emigrants from slum life. In either case, their unorganized opposition carried little weight with the much more powerful "respectable" business society.

The Housing Act of 1937 was born of the widespread unemployment during and after the Great Depression. According to Friedman:

> One significant fact of the Depression was that millions of people had left the middle class for the subsistence level or worse. People who had become used to a good standard of living were reduced to ignominious poverty. The state of affairs for the first time created a tremendous pressure for government housing—not merely for loans, not merely for a plan to prime the economic pump, but for a program for public housing designed for the needs of the decent poor. The creation of a huge, new, submerged middle class may have finally set up irresistible pressure for public housing.

Despite the new, "deserving" class of poor, the new demand for public housing was seen by some, particularly the real-estate industry, as socialism. They and others opposed public housing because it supposedly created an unlimited demand for subsidized shelter for higher and higher income groups and destroyed the incentive inherent in a free-enterprise system. Opponents charged that "if the human being is ingenious and industrious enough, he can create a house and claim it as his own. If he is careless enough to let the government do it for him, he will live in this kind of walled enclosure which compulsory state socialism affords—public housing for those who serve political masters."[7] This type of thinking contributed significantly to the form and image public housing was to take, and it provided the rationalization for the total lack of amenities in most early public-housing projects. It also served as a self-fulfilling prophecy. By not competing with the private housing market and by eliminating what were considered "frills"—for example, good landscaping, well-equipped play areas, varied building forms—it was possible to show that subsidized housing looked like prison structures. That public housing merely reflected "polite" society's view of the poor as sinful or as criminal because they had not found a way to build or own their own homes, and therefore were considered undeserving of housing that provided psychological support as well as shelter, was conveniently ignored.

The concept that government housing should be restricted from competing with private housing was fostered by the business stagnation and low profits of the depression and the real-estate industry's fear (notwithstanding a fervent belief in "free enterprise") of competition. The National Association of Real Estate Boards favored federal support for mortgage insurance in order to stimulate home ownership and home sales, but they bitterly opposed public housing because they feared it might "discourage" ownership by setting up competition individuals could not meet or because it might make "tenement occupancy so attractive that the urge to buy one's own home would be diminished."[8]

Consequently, in order to pass the 1937 Housing Act proponents of the legislation felt it was necessary to confine the program to construction of housing only for those who could not afford what private enterprise was willing and able to build. The "ideal" housing act was considered one that would accept the new poor (the submerged middle class) and reject the old poor; it would shut the doors with the ability to get housing privately, and it would not open the doors to people on the dole and likely to stay there. Housing experts believed that the requirement of rental sufficient to meet expenses would tend to restrict public housing to the honest, working poor. Hopefully, the projects would be filled with deserving but underpaid workers—innocent victims of economic reverses who needed a "break" to tide them over the lean years.[9] Part of the provision of the act was that residency was restricted to families whose net income did not exceed five times the rental, and Congress specifically provided that no annual contribution from the federal government would be given unless the local agency had demonstrated that a gap of at least 20 percent had been left between upper rental limits for admission to the proposed low-rent housing and the lowest rents that private enterprise was providing. A sage commentator noted that this provision guaranteed that there would always be a segment of the population for whom neither the government nor private enterprise provided housing.[10]

This very brief history of public-housing legislation indicates how accurately public housing, as a whole, has embodied the values, ideals, contradictions, and philosophy of those who created it. It also indicates just as accurately how there was never any real possibility that such "public" housing, associated as it was with "socialism" and perceived as a threat to private enterprise, would have even attempted to produce housing that reflected the values and ideals

Figure 3-1
Early public housing was meant to be a temporary way-station for the submerged middle class. It reflected society's attitude that public housing should discourage its residents from wanting to live there indefinitely.

of those who would inhabit it. Public housing took the form it did because of certain values and moral and economic reasons and not from a lack of information about people's values and desired housing images. The act was written to reflect the ideas of those who wished to ensure that the "unworthy" poor won no undeserved benefits. The houses were built to be sturdy, functional, cheap, and plain. No one stopped to consider that attractive urban architecture benefits everyone. Public housing was simply supposed to act as a way station for the temporarily dispossessed. It was to be a "slum of hope" without peeling plaster and nauseous privies.[11] It was created to stigmatize its occupants as different from and inferior to those who could purchase housing from commercial developers.

Against this historical background of public housing, the effort the New York State Urban Development Corporation made between 1968 and 1975 to provide not only a large quantity of public-housing units but housing units that were of high quality and, from the user's perspective, undistinguishable from privately developed and owned units, is worth describing.

The UDC was a unique agency in terms of its power and size. It was a state agency and public benefit corporation created by the New York State legislature in 1968 to develop and finance housing for low- and moderate-income families; to assist industrial and commercial development; and to provide needed educational, cultural, and other civic facilities. As a general rule, UDC residential developments were built for a mix of moderate- and middle-income families (70 percent), low-income families (20 percent), and low-income elderly persons (10 percent). UDC used a variety of federal and state assistant programs to achieve this goal. Its projects were designed by private architects and consultants and built by private firms and individuals. UDC acted chiefly as a catalyst; it assumed responsibility for providing much of the development package itself and for dealing with other governmental agencies. Its goal was to eliminate as much as possible red tape often caused by the division of responsibility among various levels of government and among various agencies within the same level of government. To accomplish this it was given the power by the state Legislature to acquire land by condemnation and to waive local zoning ordinances. Although these powers were not used, they elicited tremendous hostility and resentment from communities that feared their autonomy was seriously jeopardized. UDC's effectiveness in getting housing units built is illustrated by the fact that at the end of 1972, when the federal government severely curtailed its housing subsidy programs, UDC had started more than 30,000 housing units in 101 different projects in 44 communities.

The UDC collapsed financially, along with the rest of New York City, at a time when its building activity had already been curtailed by the reduction of federal and state housing money. It is too soon to measure the impact that the UDC will have on future public housing. The UDC was intended as a model program and organization, and it left several specific prototypes that may serve as models for future public housing.

Its most tangible achievement may be the design and construction of low-rise, high-density housing in Brooklyn, New York.[12]

This housing is significant because it represents a very real attempt to move away from high-rise towers that are impersonal, isolate families from each other, and eliminate any possibility of easy access between apartment and ground-level activities for children. All spaces in the four-story prototypes are clearly identified as private, semiprivate, semipublic, and public. Almost all units have a private outdoor space, either a garden or balcony, and outdoor public areas and porches are organized to provide control over who may enter. Each apartment is oriented so that either the living or dining space has a view to the street or to the private garden. This reinforces surveillance over the street, allows supervision of children, and brings sunlight and cross-ventilation into each apartment. All the entrances are private or semiprivate and located directly on the street. Inside the apartment, bedrooms have been acoustically separated as much as possible from living areas by halls or baths or by their location on another level.

These prototypical units are not the first low-rise, high-density housing to be designed, but they do represent one of the first attempts at public housing in the United States where the main consideration has been directed toward housing families economically and humanely in a densely organized community. This housing is also significant because it represents one of the few times a large development company has utilized behavioral science research findings as a basis for architectural design.

Those involved in the project made every attempt to base decisions, and trade-offs, on empirical data concerned with how people wanted to live, not merely on convenience or simple economics. The use of behavioral science data as a means of creating humane housing whose design could be supported on something more than the personal predilections and values of an architect or developer was reflected in the tremendous time and energy the UDC architecture staff, under the direction of Theodore Liebman, devoted to the development of design criteria. These criteria, based on empirical studies done in Britain, the United States, and other countries, attempted to outline the organization, arrangement, and use of space at both the site and apartment level by defining the need, type, amount, and appropriate locations of public and private facilities and amenities necessary to support certain activities. These criteria became unwieldy, and yet they provided a checklist of user requirements and some answers to questions infrequently or never previously asked in designing and building public housing.

UDC's ability to control all aspects of the building program, from design and construction to management, demonstrated the importance of viewing a housing development holistically: the best-designed spaces will become dilapidated slums unless the management of the facilities is as closely planned as the design. Although all the developments were managed by private companies, UDC maintained a central management division and regional offices. The central office dictated policy and hired and fired the private management companies. The management, architecture, and construction divisions were influential in determining where money would be spent to make repairs or major postconstruction changes, such as enclosing an exposed ground-level parking

44   *Housing Messages*

Figure 3-2
Public housing does not have to stigmatize its occupants or be a visual blight on the community. UDC developments (a and b) are indistinguishable from upper income private developments and reflect the attitude that low income groups want and need the same type of housing as any other income group.

Public Housing 45

c

d

46   Housing Messages

e

f

area with chain-link fence and electronically controlled gates to provide better security.

The centralization of management in terms of basic policy enabled UDC as a developer to coordinate its total package and to ensure, as much as possible, that careful work in the design and construction stages was not negated once the project was completed and in its first crucial months of operation. It also made the day-to-day running of the developments difficult for the on-site managers, and in several cases generated conflict between them and the director of management at UDC. Ideally, UDC staff might have made a greater effort to delegate responsibilities to the on-site manager and to explain the reasons for their policies.

These developments were difficult to manage because UDC was trying to cater to different income, age, and racial groups simultaneously: black, white, Spanish, and other racial and ethnic groups; low- and moderate-income groups; and the elderly and large numbers of children. Many private management companies, and the managers themselves, would be overwhelmed trying to cope with such diverse groups and the problems stemming from their interaction. Most private management firms are geared to collecting rent, maintaining the facilities, and doing minor repair work. UDC's management staff attempted to hire staff that could help the private management companies deal with some of the more difficult management problems more effectively. Through their field representatives the central management tried to keep close enough to the situation to make informed decisions. They did not always succeed.

For example, the attempt to improve security at one of the New York City sites by simply increasing the number of guards failed because it did not deal with the reasons *any* guards were ineffective. Fining children for playing on the grass and erecting fences across user-made paths as a means of maintaining the appearance of a development did not alter the "undesirable" behavior and made some children resentful. Despite UDC's intentions, most of the guidance UDC provided to the on-site management was oriented toward ameliorating administrative and fiscal, rather than social problems.

The genuine interest in the welfare of the actual users of the built environment was also reflected in UDC's live-in program, and their sponsorship of the *Design for Living* report noted in Chapter 2. The live-in program was developed by UDC staff members to provide the division heads with feedback and insight into how completed developments were actually functioning. UDC executives and their families lived in UDC housing for one to two weeks and then in a written report described their experiences and observations. These written reports were widely circulated within the organization and in some cases became informal design criteria. This program represented a major departure from the usual procedure in building houses for low- and moderate-income groups. It is rare in this country for those who design and build such housing to have ever experienced what it is like to actually live there, even for a short period of time. Implicitly, this live-in program also revealed a radical assumption: housing for low- and moderate-income people should be evaluated using the same criteria applied to middle- and upper-middle income housing.

The amount and validity of the information collected through informal procedures during a one- or two-week stay in a strange environment is necessarily limited. As part of its ongoing interest in making the rationale for design decisions explicit and basing these on behavioral data rather than whimsy or personal experience alone, UDC decided to sponsor in the fall of 1972 a more rigorous, in-depth evaluation of their completed housing developments. Their *Design for Living* report is the outgrowth of that research and represents an example of user evaluation research that could serve as a model for other housing authorities. This is particularly true since the research instruments developed could be (and were) used by UDC's own staff to evaluate their housing developments.

The research objectives for the UDC study were general. A number of different UDC housing developments, primarily in urban areas, were to be evaluated to discover what residents (including adults, teenagers, the elderly, and children) felt about the housing provided by UDC and the ways in which they were using it. The study focused on two levels of the residential environment: (1) the dwelling unit and (2) the development (site itself). The focus was on how people use and perceive their environment, including its management, and not on the technology of building construction or the economics of housing construction per se unless it directly affected the occupants' reactions. These factors obviously influence the product with which residents must cope, but a specific investigation of these factors was beyond the scope of the study.

Details of the methods used and the rationale for using them can be found in the original report *Design for Living: The Residents' View of Multifamily Housing*.[13] Briefly, data were collected from seven different UDC developments (three high-rise and 4 low-rise) in urban and suburban areas throughout New York State, ranging from the South Bronx in New York City to Binghamton and Niagara Falls in upstate New York. An additional UDC development was used to pretest the instruments. Four separate research instruments were developed: (1) resident interview, (2) questionnaire checklist, (3) systematic observation, and (4) management interviews. In addition, interviewers talked casually with residents and on-site management and recorded their observations.

On the average, interviews were conducted in 25 percent of the total number of occupied units in each development. The refusal rate was less than 10 percent for personal interviews, and the return rate for questionnaires ranged from 26 percent to 59 percent, with an average return rate of 44 percent. The total sample size consisted of 357 randomly selected resident interviews, which averaged approximately an hour in length, 591 completed questionnaire checklists, nearly 100 observation periods, and interviews with all on-site managers. An additional 41 questionnaires were completed with teenagers, plus many casual conversations with them.

This study, in combination with the attempt to develop detailed design criteria for living requirements and the low-rise, high-density project in Brooklyn, was to culminate in the Roosevelt Island design competition sponsored by UDC.[14] This was a major competition that, probably for the first time, had very explicit user requirements that had to be met and described by competitors. At the time of the competition in April 1976, UDC had essentially collapsed, and there was no longer any guarantee that the winning entries would be built.

The competition was conceived as an opportunity to educate architects about livability criteria as much as it was an attempt to get the best housing available for the site. The fact that almost three hundred architects paid homage to criteria other than novel form, even superficially, represented a fairly successful attempt to change the direction of architecture as it applies to multifamily, and particularly public, housing. Not building the winning design will just as surely weaken the value of such a direction in some architects' minds.

UDC was not perfect. No organization is. What distinguishes it from most other large bureaucracies is that it tried to learn from its mistakes. As an organization, it was certainly political, but its political image was predicated on its providing, in quantity, quality housing for low- and moderate-income groups. It did not change any of the underlying assumptions about the mechanism for providing public housing to the poor and near poor, but did change the assumption about what public housing should be, in the sense that it was clearly and unambiguously intended not to stigmatize its occupants, but to give them quality housing that supported the occupants' goals and values. It is this aspect of UDC that can serve as the most useful model for future public housing.

REFERENCES

1. R. Fisher, *Twenty Years of Public Housing: Economic Aspects of the Federal Program* (New York: Harper and Brothers, 1959).
2. L. Friedman, *Government and Slum Housing: A Century of Frustration* (Chicago: Rand McNally and Co., 1968).
3. Ibid.
4. J. Riis, *How the Other Half Lives* (New York: Hill and Wang, 1957), p. 6.
5. Friedman, *Government and Slum Housing,* p. 25.
6. Ibid.
7. Fisher, *Twenty Years,* p. 9.
8. Friedman, *Government and Slum Housing,* p. 105.
9. Ibid.
10. Ibid., p. 111.
11. Ibid., p. 113.
12. "Low-Rise High-Density: UDC/IAUS Publicly Assisted Housing," *Progressive Architecture* (December 1973).
13. F. D. Becker, *Design for Living: The Residents' View of Multifamily Housing* (Ithaca, N.Y.: Center for Urban Development Research, Cornell University, 1974).
14. "This Side of Habitat: Roosevelt Island Housing Competition," *Progressive Architecture* (July 1975): 58-63.

4

Personalization

> The furniture we install, the way we arrange it, the pictures we hang, the plants we buy and tend, all are expressions of our images of ourselves, all are messages about ourselves that we want to convey back to ourselves, and to the few intimates that we invite into this, our house.
>
> C. Cooper, *"The House as Symbol of Self"*[1]

Many researchers have described how animals define their territorial boundaries by using a characteristic "marker."[2] For some species this is olfactory; for others it is visual or auditory. These markers differentiate space according to individual and group ownership, and their effectiveness depends on a shared definition of what constitutes a marker. Similar types of marking behavior seem to occur among humans: building fences, gates, hedges, putting names on doors. While most marking behaviors among animal species are directed at discouraging unwanted intruders, in human populations they more often may incorporate a self-expressive function. We often do not build just any fence; we build one we like, which in some way reflects our own values, notions of beauty, status, creativity, or skill. Personalization reinforces the occupant's own sense of identity, as well as expresses it to others, and it is a way of demonstrating to others that the space is occupied by someone in particular. Personalization, unlike people's art and other aspects of folk art and user participation—which are generally characterized by the anonymity of the persons who created the product—is individually (or group) identifiable.[3]

Personalization sets the stage for interaction. By providing information about the individual to those within the territory, the owner/occupant influences the type of interaction that occurs and indicates certain roles or topics as appropriate or inappropriate. Chicanos or black persons who hang political posters emphasizing their group's strength and power is signaling that they expect to be treated with dignity and respect. Clear communication of territorial claims is advantageous both to the occupant and to the receiver. The occupant can develop a "place" with which to identify and from which he or she can send messages about status, class, prestige, values, political ideology, and taste with the knowledge that the conditions he or she places upon behavior within the territory will be recognized and respected. The receiver is informed of the behavior pattern expected and can reasonably decide on appropriate courses of action.

MEANING OF PERSONALIZATION

Studies of marking behavior in humans have shown that the more personal an object used as a marker is (the more individually identifiable), the more effective that marker is in protecting that space. In early studies done in library and cafeteria settings, personal books, papers, and articles of clothing were more effective in delaying occupancy and controlling the space than were less personal objects such as library books, newspapers, or sandwiches. In a college library setting, people perceived books and other personal objects left on tables and chairs as representing persons in absentia, and they reacted to these markers in a way analogous to the way they would react to a person sitting there: they avoided sitting at a marked table if unmarked and unoccupied tables were available, and they almost never sat at a marked place under any circumstances.[4] Even if the impression outsiders gain from personalization is incorrect, their very acknowledgment of individuality makes it more difficult for an outsider to look at the owner as being an anonymous individual whose space can be casually invaded.[5]

The fact that "appearance" and "the ability to make changes outside" have been found to be important predictors of satisfaction for public-housing residents suggests that people compensate for low status, expressed through physical cues, by creating their own environmental messages.[6] The appearance of most public housing, as noted in chapter 3, stigmatizes those who live in it as inferior. The desire to personalize the exterior of one's apartment is a logical way for residents to personally disassociate themselves from the overall image of the project. By spending time, money, and effort to improve the outside appearance of their individual units, a family can proclaim its individuality and counteract the largely negative message the building itself conveys about the residents, both to themselves and to all those who pass by it. Fewer instances of personalization occur in high-income apartments where the building itself conveys high status, respectability, and worth. The resident has no need to counteract the building's environmental messages.

In one of the few systematic studies focusing directly on personalization, Hansen found that among male college freshmen living in joint occupancy in dormitory rooms that most personalization involved nonintimate forms of decoration, such as abstract decoration and objects related to entertainment and personal interest.[7] These students seemed to be trying to create an atmosphere that was socially acceptable, functional, and visually stimulating. Personalization by roommates generally involved the use of items that followed common themes or were in similar categories of personalization. Over time the particular objects a student used changed, but the type of object remained relatively stable. In a recent study of married student housing it was found that occupants modified the living environment for themselves and to communicate to others their own values and life-style.[8]

In the absence of more systematic information about what constitutes personalization and the meaning it has for those who engage in it, especially outside dormitory settings, Coniglio undertook a small study using a multifamily housing development in Ithaca, New York, occupied by moderate- and low-income persons.[9] She interviewed forty-one residents, 71 percent of whom were student families. The majority were between twenty-one and thirty years old. Eighty percent of the persons interviewed were women, and 24 percent were foreign students. The population characteristics were largely determined by the development's proximity to a large university.

Not surprisingly, most residents felt that part of a home is being surrounded by one's own things, and about half the residents said a place felt like home after personalization had occurred. Over 90 percent said the first thing they did to make a new place comfortable and homelike was some act of personalization. Almost 70 percent of the residents said that personalization was essential or very important, and only 5 percent said it was unimportant.

There were several different ways in which personalization of residential interiors could be achieved, and most residents used more than one way. Placing objects with special meaning in the environment was the most common means of personalizing their living space. Personalized objects such as handmade wall hangings or a particular chair had some emotional significance, but the basis for this differed. One resident felt that the "fact that we made it was really important or even the fact that it was handed down." Others mentioned only that the object should reflect their own individuality in some way: "Used stuff but still reflects my taste" or "That's me." The emotional connotation of objects was very important to their owners. A functional object without emotional attributes had no intrinsic value, and owners would leave them behind rather than bother moving them to a new residence.

As one means of expressing one's own values and individuality, aesthetic objects were an important component of personalization. *Aesthetic* was defined by each individual and not by anything approaching a norm. Many residents felt they understood what was considered "aesthetic" in architectural or design terms, but they felt a designer's concept of aesthetic had little meaning for them—after all, they knew what they liked! Objects used to personalize an interior carried emotional meanings to their owners beyond their territorial marking function.

A less obvious means of expressing individuality and personal values was housekeeping (the large proportion of female respondents may have affected these results). For example, nearly 80 percent of the residents sampled disliked the white walls, and of those reacting negatively, 67 percent did so because the walls were difficult to keep clean. For many residents the cleanliness of the home is a reflection on the family and, more particularly, on the wife. Cleaning becomes an act of personalization ("so they think at least I'm a decent housekeeper"). These findings were supported by the UDC study, which found that keeping apartments neat and clean was a way of indicating respectability to friends, relatives, and strangers. Residents became frustrated and discouraged attempting to clean walls and other surfaces that resisted their efforts.

In Coniglio's study the arrangement of furniture was perceived as personalization by the resident sample since most residents wanted to "do something different from everybody else." Discussions with residents suggested that personalization is a continuing process in which objects are continuously added and deleted. Since personalization reinforces and reflects one's identity, it was not surprising that the nature of the objects selected changed as the person's financial resources and self-image continued to evolve. The freedom to manipulate their living space seemed to be important for several reasons—functional requirements, need for change and variety, the ability to express individuality, and the desire to feel that one has the power to control a piece of the world.

CONCEPTUAL FRAMEWORK

No single theory or conceptual framework exists to explain why people seem to engage in personalization or attempt to manipulate their environment in ways that reflect themselves, their values, and their individuality. Perin has applied White's theory of competence to environmental design in general, and it is useful in trying to understand personalization.[10] White developed the concept *sense of competence* within the framework of psychoanalytic theory because he felt a complete theory had to incorporate growth processes depending on exploration and manipulation, which in turn facilitated the integration of "man's complex repertory of adaptive behavior." According to White, "Competence is the cumulative result of the history of interactions with the environment. Sense of competence is suggested as a suitable term for the subjective side of this, signifying one's consciously or unconsciously felt competence—one's confidence—in dealing with the various aspects of the environment."[11] Within this framework, personalization, or manipulation of one's microenvironment, is part of the process of growth of one's general sense of mastery and control.

Joachim Wohlwill has drawn on the experimental work done by Berlyn and others on stimulus seeking, stimulus exploration, and the complexity of environmental stimuli to explain reactions to different environmental configurations.[12] Paralleling early studies done with children, Wohlwill found that responses to photographic slides of the physical environment vary as a function of the judged complexity of these scenes. Wohlwill related the linear relationship between the amount of voluntary exploratory activity and the stimuli complexity, and the fact that evaluative or affective responses reach an optimal value at a low or intermediate level of complexity, to Berlyn's distinction between exploratory activity directed at information seeking and that directed at affective arousal. Residents' desire to personalize their living environment, which increases its complexity and stimulates "exploratory" behavior, may be an expression of their own need for certain levels of environmental complexity. This may be particularly true in drab and uniform dormitory rooms or motel-like apartment buildings.

People are not seeking levels of stimulation per se but rather levels of stimulation that have specific meaning for them and have reinforcement and reflection of identity as central functions. The application of theories of stimulus-seeking behavior, which relate exploration of and attention to facets of the environment to specific physical and social cues, seems more appropriate to impersonal aspects of public environments that we must experience but that do not necessarily have to reflect a group or individual identity, at least for those only passing through that environment. Airports, bus terminals, and public lobbies are good examples. Personalization also involves participation at some level, whereas environmental complexity can be achieved without the users' participation, for example, the design of a park, lobby, or exterior facade.

Another concept useful in understanding residents' negative reaction to restrictions on personalizing their own room or apartment is Brehm's concept of "psychological reactance" and its relationship to territoriality.[13] The essential behavioral and psychological component of territory is the individual's or group's freedom to control the activities and determine appropriate behavior within a specific spatial area. In a number of attitude change experiments, Brehm has shown that people react to a threat or actual loss of freedom to believe in a particular way by becoming more negative or taking an attitude position different from one they might choose in the absence of pressure to make a particular choice. To the extent that a housing development's or dormitory's relationship to the residents, expressed through management personnel, policies, and physical design, is perceived as restricting behavior alternatives—reducing freedom of choice—residents may become more negative or act in more unusual ways than they would if they felt they were free from pressures or expectations to behave in a certain way. Restrictions do not necessarily involve the physical impossibility of an activity; they can occur through subtle attitudes and by the difficulty required for certain behaviors or activities to occur.

The above discussion suggests that some of the reasons people engage in personalization are that it makes manifest individual and group differences and reinforces one's sense of individual or group identity; it increases the complexity of the environment and fulfills the need for exploratory stimulation; and it facilitates the development of a sense of competence and mastery, which is important to personal growth. Restrictions to personalization are reacted to negatively because they limit the above activities and because they are perceived, consciously or unconsciously, as conflicting with implicit norms about what an individual can do in a personal or group territory.

CONSEQUENCES AND FUNCTIONS OF PERSONALIZATION

Much of the apparently willful destruction of the physical environment seems to be preceded by the perception that administrators, managers, or designers do not care about, or are even hostile to, the persons living in the setting. Restrictions on modifying, personalizing, or planning environments are significant means of conveying this lack of concern, intentionally or unintentionally. From this perspective, vandalism can be viewed as an environmental message that informs others about what residents think of such restrictions and those responsible for their creation and enforcement. Yet individual alteration of the physical environments is not always destructive; it can represent a positive interaction with the immediate environment in an attempt to make it more responsive to particular living habits and life-style. The study by Phillip Boudon mentioned earlier, in which occupants of Quarters Modernes Fruges at Le Pessac, France, decreased the discrepancy between the cubist style of the buildings and the traditional regional forms, is one example of families' making their individual living environments more responsive to ideal images of home and preferred life-styles.[14]

In a more journalistic than scientific investigation, Bush-Brown described and documented the Garden Club of Philadelphia's implementation of community "garden blocks" by providing designs for flower boxes and help in constructing them.[15] Supported by some striking before and after photographs, she described the effects of introducing gardens and flower boxes into what she described as apathetic, blighted, and deteriorated neighborhoods. The goal was to stimulate a sense of neighborhood pride in areas where it had long since disappeared. According to Bush-Brown, the results were overwhelmingly positive: neighborhoods began to sprout colorful flowers and miniparks, neighbors started to talk to each other, residents began to maintain other parts of their block not directly related to the flowers, and people began to use the streets again. The garden blocks became a form of both individual and group (neighborhood) personalization and pride, which stimulated group cohesiveness.

In a study of dorms at Berkeley, personalization (the rearrangement possibilities of furniture and the ability to hang things on the walls) was an important factor in creating dorm livability. Within the context of mental institutions, Osmond has described the need for allowing patients to express their individuality by personalizing their own living space.[16] Many mentally disturbed persons are not sure who or where they are, and impersonal institutional environments exacerbate these feelings and are contrary to the purpose of the institution.

In a more systematic behavioral study in a college dormitory, Eigenbrod related social-group compatibility and territoriality to identity, security, academic achievement, disciplinary differences, satisfaction with room, and satisfaction with roommates.[17] He divided 208 volunteer undergraduates, 81 males and 127 females, into groups. One of the groups had complete freedom to manipulate their environment (room), including unlimited use of tape on the walls, the use of safe appliances, and the freedom to add or remove furniture and to rearrange it. The other group lived with more restrictive rules. Subjects' self-reports were used to measure identity and security.

Greater freedom was not significantly related to identity, security, or academic achievement, but it was significantly related to satisfaction with the residence hall and satisfaction with the roommate. Other consequences of the increased freedom included less damage to the hall, fewer disciplinary referrals, improved relationships between residents and advisers, establishment of more group cooperation and identity, more creative decoration of rooms, decoration of lounges, and better student maintenance of dorms.

The impetus for increasing student involvement in dormitories and making them more similar to apartments in terms of the freedom students are allowed in them was not an altruistic gesture on the part of college administrators. Administrators were faced with forty-year mortgages, which they were unable to meet as students moved out of these buildings in increasingly large numbers.[18] Increasing student involvement in the management and administration of dormitories, including both their design and allocation of financial resources, has resulted in reduced vandalism and increased student satisfaction.[19] At Ithaca College, with a student body of fewer than 6,000, $22,000 was needed to repair or replace damaged property in dormitories and other campus buildings in 1971. After implementing policies that increased students' financial responsibility and personal freedom, property damage has decreased nearly 50 percent, although vandalism is still a major problem.[20]

The opportunity to participate conveys, in itself, administrators' positive image of students, as well as increasing the probability that design decisions, which participants now have a stake in, are more reflective of the users' life-styles and habits. At MIT the least desirable dormitory on campus was completely revamped by architects working in conjunction with students living in that dormitory; it became the most popular dormitory on campus, even for students who had not participated in its development.[21]

In describing some of the frustration, anger, and dissatisfaction that occurs under conditions of restricted freedom of expression and choice, an important mitigating factor is residents' expectations about what apartment or dormitory living entails. In Coniglio's exploratory study, we found that residents' frustrations stemming from restrictions on activities (more than personalization in the sense of decoration) were mediated by their low expectations for apartment living and their relatively short and well-defined anticipated length of residence.

INTERIOR VERSUS EXTERIOR PERSONALIZATION

The meaning and consequences of interior personalization (within an apartment or dormitory room) seem quite different from exterior personalization in semiprivate areas (porches, backyards, front yards, and so on). What we do to the inside of our homes is known only to ourselves, some friends, and relatives. The community, other residents in relative proximity, has no visible indication of each other's pride and involvement in their residence and neighborhood. The possibility of social facilitation or group conformity processes operating, in which some residents are encouraged, by example, to take pride in their neighborhood or to take the trouble to improve the appearance of their "territory," is much reduced. Bush-

Brown's study seemed to indicate that exterior personalization significantly increased the feeling of community and "connectedness" among proximate neighbors. Considering the general apathy that exists in many high-density residential settings, with residents perceiving themselves as respectable but their neighbors as "unsavory characters," encouraging individual and group exterior personalization seems a potentially useful way of allowing residents to get to know each other and break down some of their unfounded stereotypes of each other.[22]

Particularly in public areas, it is also a way of reflecting the diversity and vitality of a city. Gyorgy Kepes argues that redirecting interest toward differentiation (in the cityscape) would inevitably bring qualities of visual distinction to the fore because our current multiplication of identical units adds no visual richness.[23] Personalization, especially of exterior semipublic areas in apartment complexes and even in commercial buildings, is one means of increasing visual differentiation for pedestrians and bicyclists, as well as helping occupants assert their uniqueness, and it does not invariably result in visual chaos.

Sommer has raised the question, along with city planners, architects, and community groups, about the extent to which each person's freedom to create his or her own environment is detrimental to overall environmental quality.[24] He essentially agrees that in an anarchist system, where everyone builds or decorates as they please according to a doctrine of short-range gain, that the quality of the environment would deteriorate rapidly. Yet Sommer feels that to be human means to create as well as to choose, and user participation in environmental decisions is necessary for an acceptable quality of life. Rather than eliminate planning, Sommer suggests planning for freedom by providing a "loose fit" between form and function. However creative and comprehensive a master plan might be, it should still leave opportunity for individual consumers to exercise options in creating environments that suit their needs. The recent move in New York City away from citywide master plans to individual plans developed by local community groups is a step toward more responsive environmental planning. At a smaller scale, the use of modular furniture and the freedom to modify rooms with partitions in dormitories at Hampshire College in Massachusetts (the partitions are used to create private bedrooms by sacrificing common living space) provides a similar type of "loose fit," which encourages individual and group expression of differences.

FACILITATING OR DISCOURAGING PERSONALIZATION

Management regulations that permit painting, hanging objects, and adding storage space or fences and design decisions that increase the flexibility of the space through movable walls, modular components, and sufficient space to arrange furniture in more than one arrangement are some of the more obvious factors facilitating personalization.

Less obvious may be the size of the community in which an individual is located. In very small communities where all members

Figure 4-1
Long corridors provide no clues about human habitation.

of the community know each other and individualization occurs through face-to-face contact, personalization may be relatively unimportant as a device for reflecting personal images and identities. In a study of old people's homes Alan Lipman found that newcomers often sat in an unmarked unoccupied chair until other persons in the room or the "owner" of the chair returned and informed them that the chair was "occupied," even though no one was sitting in it.[25] In this case social interaction rather than environmental messages were used to convey occupancy.

Personalization of interior spaces may also be affected by one's feeling of territorial security. Oscar Newman found that increased security seemed to result in increased personalization of interior spaces.[26] Since increased security was attributed in large part to better territorial definition of exterior spaces and better maintenance and pride in semiprivate outdoor areas, it seems possible that the visibility of some community pride and respectability among individual residents increased the commitment to that community and helped to break down residents' stereotypes of each other to the point where they were willing to interact with each other within their apartments. With increased social interaction inside apartments it seems reasonable that people would begin to take

60   Housing Messages

Figure 4-2
The pride, love, time, and expense involved in personalizing the interior of an apartment is invisible to next door neighbors.

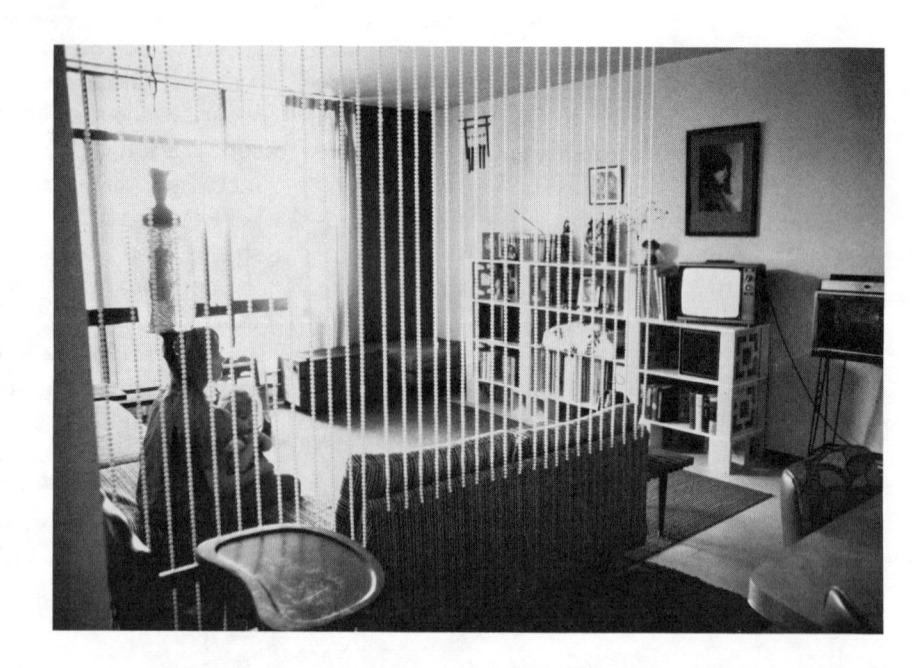

more pride in the apartment's appearance and become less fearful that time and money spent on personalizing the apartment would be negated by theft or vandalism. These types of relationships deserve further study.

The importance of design factors, such as clear delineation of semiprivate spaces, on personalization was indicated in the UDC study by the very few signs of any type of personalization found in exterior areas in high-rise buildings, in which there is no semiprivate exterior space, in contrast to low-rise developments with well-defined private entrances and/or backyards. In these latter cases people created symbolic fences, hung outdoor lighting, bought patio furniture, and created small gardens.[27] Casual observations indicated differences in the amount of personalization between units with and without clear territorial definitions, created a priori by design factors, and suggest that residents will continue the process of territorial definition through personalization, but are less likely to invest in personalization initially if it is unclear who is responsible for what spaces.

Ironically, we take a kind of schizophrenic attitude toward multifamily housing: we encourage people socially and economically to "improve" single-family houses by landscaping and painting them, adding storage space, and building patios (and the value of the property *increases* because of these modifications), and yet we actively discourage the same activities in apartment residents. We seem to assume that each new occupant of an apartment wants it returned to its original condition. People want to find a new resi-

Figure 4-3
Personalization of exterior areas provides visible clues that residents care about where they live, and is one way of making an impersonal apartment homelike.

Personalization 63

Figure 4-4
Neighbors' opinions can be an effective force in keeping exterior personalization within the community's accepted standards. The expression of concern is authentic even if the stone is not.

dence clean and well maintained, but we know of no evidence indicating that it should look exactly like all other apartments. In a study of paint policies at the University of California at Davis, the repaint ratio of personalized rooms was only 10 percent, and the cost of maintenance was substantially reduced by having students paint their own rooms.[28]

In a study I am just beginning now, pilot test data suggest that students in dormitories are often very eager and willing to be able to move into a room that a previous occupant has modified. What is interesting about these preliminary data is that students seem more receptive to major structural changes, like adding lofts to rooms with high ceilings, than they are to more "decorative" alterations, like painting. The former type of structural changes seems to result in better living spaces, from a functional standpoint, while leaving a minimal amount of the previous resident's personal identity. The latter alterations improve the space minimally at best from a purely functional standpoint, while leaving strong traces of the previous occupant's personality. Students want a room to have "personality" but not one so pervasive it restricts their own personal imprint. If further data collection and analysis support the preliminary findings, it should result in some rethinking about the assumption that each successive generation of students wants a room that has been main-

Personalization 65

Figure 4-5
Management's arbitrarily painting doors one of two colors does not provide diversity among identical units, give residents the opportunity to personalize their own space, or increase their feeling of belonging.

Figure 4-6
Allowing residents to choose the color combinations for the door graphics is a small step toward providing the opportunity to individualize one's apartment, but the important provision is the private front yard where residents can create their own gardens. The gardens add real diversity as well as beauty to the overall development.

tained in its original, impersonal, and stark state.

To summarize, the opportunity for personalization (participation) seems to result generally in more satisfaction for those involved in it, along with less property damage and better maintenance of physical facilities. Individual personalization efforts visible to others in the community seem to stimulate social interaction and may facilitate the breakdown of negative stereotypes residents have of each other that act as barriers to the development of a sense of community.

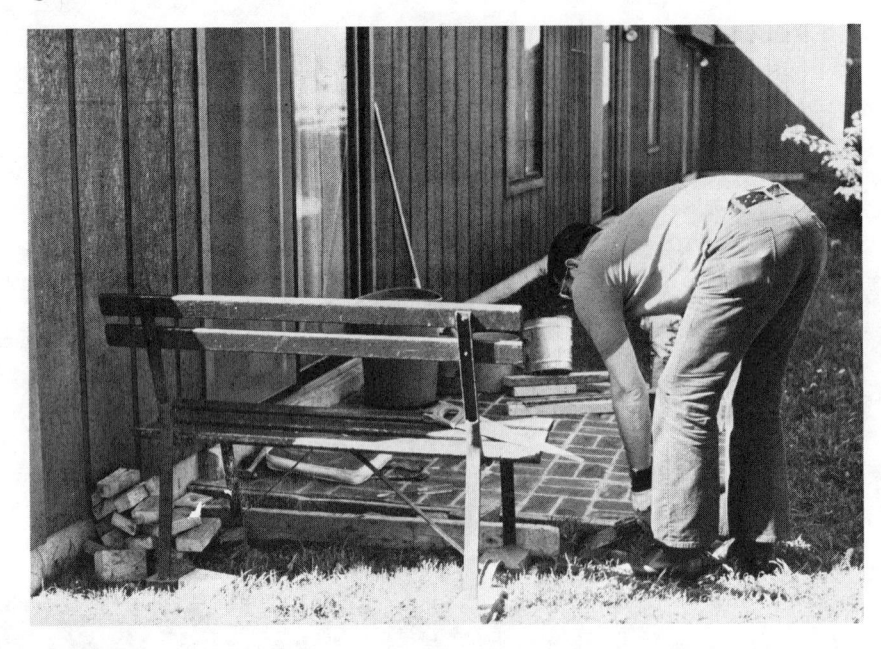

Figure 4-7
Why prohibit such activities in rental units when they are so desirable in privately owned homes? People who spend this much effort to create something will take care of it and the development will begin to look less like a motel and more like a lived-in neighborhood.

The development of a sense of competency and mastery of an environment, the need for optimal levels of environmental stimulation, the negative consequences of restrictions on our "freedom of choice" within the territorial boundaries of our homes, and the improved outcome that results from participation were suggested as conceptual frameworks for understanding why people engage in personalization and why it has the consequences it does.

Given the potential benefits that the opportunity for personalization has, we need to answer more reliably who wants to personalize and under what conditions; how physical environmental messages are decoded, and through what chain of events their impact is felt; what effects individual and group personalization have on group cohesiveness and the sense of community, and how personalization affects interaction patterns and the development of friendships. We need to develop design solutions and administrative policy that facilitate the positive effects of personalization while minimizing the chaos that might result if everyone plans their own environment without respect to anyone else.

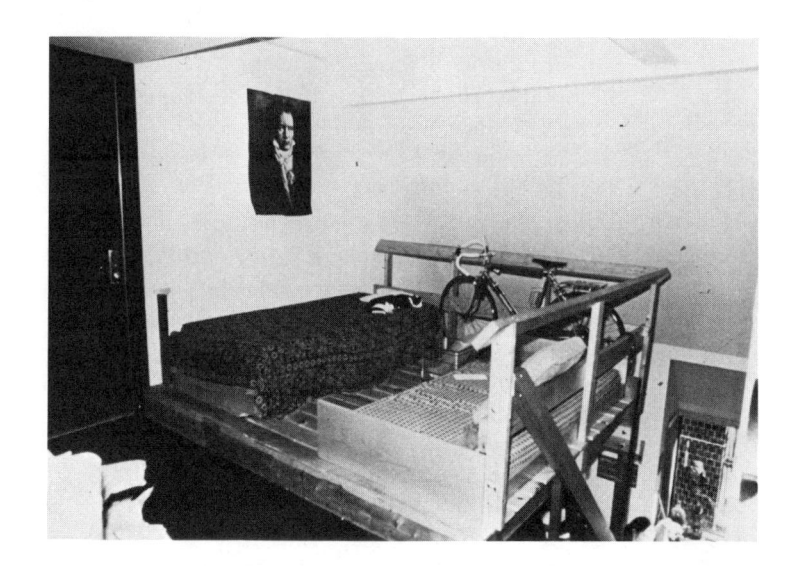

Figure 4-8
Building a loft not only makes that apartment unique, which is desirable, but it creates more usable space for the current and future occupants. There is still plenty of room for additional personalization by the next group of students.

REFERENCES

1. C. Cooper, "The House as Symbol of Self," in J. Lang et al. (eds.) *Architecture and Human Behavior* (Stroudsburg, Pa.: Dowden, Hutchinson & Ross, 1974).
2. F. D. Becker and C. Mayo, "Delineating Personal Distance and Territoriality," *Environment and Behavior* 3 (1971): 375-381; F. D. Becker, "Studies of Spatial Markers," *Journal of Personality and Social Psychology* (1973); I. Altman, *The Environment and Social Behavior* (Monterey, Calif.: Brooks/Cole Publishing Company, 1975). See also "A Conceptual Analysis," in *Environment and Behavior* 8 (March 1976): 7-30, and J. Edney, "Human Territoriality," 31 (1974): 959-975.
3. R. Sommer, "People's Art" (unpublished manuscript, 1972).
4. R. Sommer, and F. D. Becker, "Territorial Defense and the Good Neighbor," *Journal of Personality and Social Psychology* 11 (1969): 85-92.
5. E. Goffman, *Relations in Public* (New York: Harper & Row, 1971).
6. G. Francescato; S. Weidemann; J. Anderson; and R. Chenoweth, "Predictors of Satisfaction in Multi-family Housing" (working paper, Housing Research and Development Program, University of Illinois at Urbana-Champagne, 1975).
7. W. Hansen, "Personalization as a Predictor of Success and Early Termination in College" (Senior thesis, University of Utah, 1974).
8. R. Mautz, and R. Kaplan, "Residential Modification as a Mode of Self-Expression," in *Man-Environment Interaction: Evaluation and Application* (Environmental Design Research Association, 1974), 9:55-68.
9. C. Coniglio, "The Meaning of Personalization in Residential Interiors" (Master's thesis, Cornell University, 1974).
10. C. Perin, *With Man in Mind: An Interdisciplinary Prospectus for Environmental Design* (Cambridge: The MIT Press, 1970).
11. R. White, "Motivation Reconsidered: The Concept of Competence," *Psychological Review* 66 (1969): 297-333.
12. J. Wohlwill, "The Emerging Discipline of Environmental Psychology," *American Psychologist* 25 (1970): 303-312.
13. J. W. Brehm, *A Theory of Psychological Reactance* (New York: Academic Press, 1966).
14. P. Boudon, *Lived-In Architecture* (Cambridge: The MIT Press, 1969).
15. L. Bush-Brown, *Garden Blocks for Urban America* (New York: Charles Scribner's Sons, 1969).
16. S. Van Der Ryn, and M. Silverstein, *Dorms at Berkeley* (Berkeley: University of California Center for Planning and Development Research, 1967), and H. Osmond, "Function as the Basis of Psychiatric Ward Design," *Mental Hospitals* 8 (1957): 23-30.
17. F. Eigenbrod, "The Effects of Territory and Personality Compatibility on Identity and Security" (Ph.D. diss., University of Michigan, 1969).
18. M. Heilweil, "The Influence of Dormitory Architecture on Resident Behavior," *Environment and Behavior* 5 (1973): 377-412.
19. G. Jennings, "Student Damage Control at Central Michigan," *NACURH Review* (April 1972).
20. K. Perretta, "Student Vandalism on Campus," *Ithaca Journal* (January 21, 1974): 3.
21. J. Corbett, "Student-Built Housing as an Alternative to Dormitories," *Environment and Behavior* 5 (1973): 491-504.
22. C. Ankele, and R. Sommer, "The Cheapest Apartments in Town," *Environment and Behavior* 5 (1973): 505-513.
23. G. Kepes, "Notes on Expression and Communication in the Cityscape," in L. Rodwin, ed., *The Future Metropolis* (New York: George Braziller, 1961).
24. Sommer, "People's Art."
25. A. Lipman, "Building Design and Social Inter-

action: A Preliminary Study in Three Old People's Homes," *Architects Journal Information Library* 147 (1968): 23-30.
26. O. Newman, "Defensible Space" (lecture at Cornell University, May 1, 1973).
27. F. D. Becker, *Design for Living: The Residents' View of Multifamily Housing* (Ithaca, N.Y.: Center for Urban Development Research, Cornell University, 1974).
28. R. Sommer, *Tight Spaces: Hard Architecture and How to Humanize It* (Englewood Cliffs, N.J.: Prentice-Hall, 1974).

5
Participation

> Participation is inherently good; it brings people together, involves them in their world; it creates feeling between people and the world around them, because it is a world which *they* have helped to make.
>
> C. Alexander, *The Oregon Experiment*[1]

The primarily positive consequences of personalization described in the previous chapter, in terms of the participants' satisfaction with what they produce, as well as the greater willingness to maintain and defend the spaces personalized, have been attributed to participation per se as a good in itself. In addition the outcome of the product is better in the sense that it more accurately reflects the values and self-concepts of participants than if the design was created by a nonuser (although participants may realize that the finished design is not "professional" quality).

Advocacy planners and humanistic critics of architecture have argued that people need to participate in planning their own environments because it gives them a feeling of control over their environment and because participation is the only way user needs and values can really be taken into account.[2] Participation in this sense is an expression of what Alexander considers a fundamental human need to create and to control. As he says: "Whenever people have the opportunity to change the environment around them, they do it, they enjoy it, and they gain enormous satisfaction from what they have done."[3]

Not everyone feels that participation is important to user satisfaction. At one extreme of the participation debate is the "expert" position, which has been adopted by some persons in architecture, social planning, and cultural design.[4] B. F. Skinner, for example, has argued that the cultural designer, using the science of behavior, will know how to program or develop an environment that will make people creative and happy. He implies that there is no need for the people to participate directly in the decision-making process because the "expert," by virtue of educational training and understanding of people, will be able to design an environment that makes people happy and meets their needs.[5] The "expert" approach argues that it is not necessary, and is often even undesirable, for the eventual users to participate in the planning of the environment; they get in the way and lack the expertise, and participatory committees make the project much more expensive and time-consuming.

Yet it is difficult to see how outcomes that support the user's own values and lifestyle can be planned without some input, or participation, from the user during the design process. Given the current reliance on survey feedback from similar users as a basis for creating new designs, it is important for planners to learn whether indirect participation, in the form of feedback through surveys and other evaluative research that incorporates user goals and preferences in new designs, is of sufficient degree or type of participation or whether more direct participation is desirable and/or necessary.

More finely stated, we need to know who wants to participate, in what ways, on what kinds of design decisions.

Despite the importance of developing a greater understanding of the types and degrees of participation that would be most appropriately included in the design process under specific conditions, there have been few attempts to conceptually differentiate among different types of participation and to systematically investigate the effect of different types of participation on user satisfaction.

Some of the research on leadership found in the social-psychological literature relates to the issue of participation, but most of the work, particularly the initial studies, focuses on the personal qualities or human virtues of persons identified as leaders. The emphasis was on how to select good leaders and the effect of different types of leadership on group performance in meeting specific tangible goals. Very little attention was directed toward the effect of leadership in terms of subjective feelings of self-worth, satisfaction, self-esteem, or sense of competence—from either leaders or other participants' perspective.

The lack of emphasis on subjective reactions derives in large part from the definition of leadership as a "set of group functions which must occur in any group if it is to behave effectively to satisfy the needs of its members."[6] This definition focuses on the product. More recently the conceptual base for leadership studies has broadened to include an examination of the personal, environmental, and social situational variables associated with leadership.[7] Since leadership almost by definition involves active participation, looking at some of the characteristics of leaders (that is, people who participate) may be useful in increasing our understanding of the kinds of people who are likely to participate in an activity or group.

A number of different traits have been found to be associated with leadership (defined on the basis of role, sociometric choice, and so on). For short, thin people the picture is gloomy. Taller, heavier people are more often chosen and seen as leaders than short people, demonstrating in another way the influence of physical cues on social inferences. Intelligence has also been associated with leadership. Persons identified as leaders are generally higher in self-confidence, less anxious, better integrated, and have stronger willpower and perseverence than nonleaders.[8] Since most studies are correlational in nature, it is possible that these traits are as much a consequence of leadership (participation) as they are necessary prerequisites for it.

With respect to the debate over participation in the planning and design fields, none of these studies distinguishes among three critical types of participation: (1) control: the actual users participating and determining which alternative is selected; (2) input or feedback: providing opinions about what one would like to see happen but not having power to determine alternatives. This is the most common form of "citizen participation" used by city planning boards, government agencies, and so on; (3) implementation: actually producing whatever alternatives have been selected. Local community groups building their own playgrounds or remodeling a prized church or community center are common examples of this type of participation.

The political implication of each of these types of participation—in terms of the way in which power is allocated—is obvious, but the social-psychological implications are much less clear. Advocacy planners and others involved in community organization and user participation processes assume that everyone wants, or should want, responsibility for making decisions. It seems likely that many people would like to choose among alternative programs or designs and perhaps pick from alternative plans aspects that they like that can be combined in a final solution. Others might like to affect the decision-making process by having their opinions and values represented in the final decisions, while fewer people may want to actually implement the final decision. Essentially, different people like to participate in different ways, and the same person may desire to participate differently depending on how closely the decision is perceived as affecting him or her directly, his or her social status and available free time, educational background and skills level, and the type of environment in question. Rather than providing an opportunity for different types of participation, most organizers of user participation processes select the type of user participation *they* feel is most appropriate, and they ignore other types.

In addition to the kinds of problems with group participation suggested above, most participation studies have not considered situations where a product can be attained without any group participation. This is the typical situation in design, not the exception. Leadership studies, often made in industrial settings, focus on situations where group members must participate, in terms of implementing a decision, to achieve the product. Most pedestrian malls, offices, houses, schools, and hospitals are built without their users participating in any way. The users simply have to use and pay for a product others have decided is best for them.

DIFFERENT PEOPLE PARTICIPATE IN DIFFERENT WAYS

When satisfaction has been measured in leadership studies, it has been associated with economic reward and simple dominance (power/control) over other people. For example, in studies of different types of communication structures, some of which necessitate group solutions and others of which create a single leader, Leavitt found that the exercise of power, in the sense of determining the behavior of another person, was a primary determinant of satisfaction.[9] Persons who participated in the communication structure where they were dependent on a single person to make decisions were less satisfied and enjoyed the process less than those who participated in a structure where all participants had equal decision-making powers. There is evidence that some people derive vicarious satisfaction from being a participant in a group effort that achieves success,[10] but power seems to be a more important ingredient of satisfaction.

Other studies of the effects of different types of leadership, most notably between "authoritarian" and "democratic" leadership styles, have shown that when all activities are focused on a single person and when all communication must go through this person for a decision to be made, this person becomes indispensable. For the group this means that the withdrawal of the leader often leads to chaos. The limited opportunity for interpersonal communication within the group reduces morale and results in the group's being less able to withstand attack and strain. In the famous Iowa studies conducted by Lewin, Lippitt, and White in which children in a classroom situation were subjected to either a democratic or authoritarian leader, the following effects were attributed to the different leadership styles:[11]

> Authoritarian as compared to Democratic leaders produced (1) greater quantity of work, but (2) less work motivation and (3) less originality; (4) more aggressiveness to leader and group members; (5) more suppressed discontent; (6) more dependent and submissive behavior; (7) less friendliness; (8) less "group-mindedness."

Similarly when elected leaders were instructed to behave in a "participatory" manner—taking an active part in the process of group decision making and encouraging contributions from all members—or in a "supervisory" manner—seeing that the work was done but not encouraging participation—the researchers found that participatory leadership was more likely to be associated with group consensus and with participants' satisfaction with the consensus.[12] In another series of early studies done in industrial settings at the University of Michigan Institute for Social Research, researchers explored the relationship between style of leadership and work performance.[13] Their major finding was that employee-centered supervisors were higher producers than job-centered supervisors. According to Haiman, group decision making is a "powerful device for attitude and behavior change. . . . It shares decision-making and responsibility, and democratic leadership enables a group to make maximum use of the relevant individual differences existing within it."[14] Group decision making is not always more efficient.

One of the classic studies in an industrial setting that showed the advantage of "user participation" was done by Coch and French who performed a field experiment in which some of the workers in a pajama factory participated in the replanning of a production line while others implemented new plans developed by their supervisors.[15] They found greater productivity in groups that participated in the planning than those who did not. However, there was no attempt to see whether another experimental group who received the same plans as those developed by the participating workers would have been as satisfied as those who participated in the development of the plan. A form of indirect participation, in which some workers provide information that is used as a basis for designing the environments for other workers, might have been as successful as direct participation itself.

Bass and Leavitt tried to resolve this issue by comparing productivity on word game tasks in laboratory experiments between groups that developed their own plans (self-plan) and yoked groups who used plans developed by fellow workers (planned for by others).[16] Thus, plan quality was held constant, and participation in the planning process was varied. The results showed that the self-planned groups generally had significantly greater productivity than the planned-for groups. There were positive but statistically insignificant trends indicating that the self-plan groups were more satisfied with the plans and the task and felt more responsibility for the work than did the planned-for groups. These results provide support for the hypotheses that participation leads to greater morale and productivity. However, the tasks involved sentence production in number games and may have little bearing on participation in the real work situation or in the development of an actual living environment.

Since most studies that have looked at effects of participation and leadership style have been conducted in settings where a strict authoritarian hierarchy is generally accepted—the military, industry, and schools —and not in situations where people would normally expect to control decisions over their activities, such as in the home, it is difficult to generalize the leadership study findings.

In a study more closely related to environmental design Judy Corbett evaluated the reactions of students who volunteered to participate in a project to design and build individual dome dormitories.[17] The students chose the dome they wanted, its exterior color, and its location, and they designed and constructed the interiors. The most common reason students gave for their involvement was that it gave them a chance to express their individuality by designing and creating a unique room. The students tended to be very satisfied with the dormitories, and their ratings of the physical and social amenities were generally higher than ratings of students who lived in other on-campus or off-campus housing. The students also felt that it had been a very good experience, and they acquired new skills. Various architects and architectural students criticized the dormitories for being unaesthetic and crude in design, and the county planning commission called them "unsightly igloos," which they felt should not be encouraged.

Although the housing was favorably rated by the students who built it, it is not clear whether the favorable ratings were due to the students' participation in their design or to the actual qualities of the housing. In addition, it is unclear how new students would like living in these individually designed rooms. As in many other organizational behavior studies, participation and quality of the environment were confounded. Therefore the effects of each on satisfaction could not be determined.

At MIT, a team of architects and student consultants planned to renovate an old dormitory and then submitted their design suggestions to the whole dormitory for approval before implementing the changes. The dormitory climbed from the least desired to the most desired place on campus after the renovations were completed.[18] Participation and quality of the environment were not separated, but the fact that students who had not directly participated in the renovation found it very desirable suggests that direct participation may not be necessary for high levels of user satisfaction if potential users are presented with a high quality of environment that is congruent with their life-style and activity patterns.

The tremendous market for old farmhouses and almost any well-built older home suggests that there are certain qualities in people's living environments that can be satisfied by a wide range of very different structures, none of which was directly influenced by the participant. There is no evidence I know of that suggests that the majority of people are interested in completely designing and constructing their own living environments. But there is an abundance of evidence that people very much want to be able to select their living environment from a range of possibilities and want to be able to modify and personalize their living environment in an effort to make it more compatible with their own life-style and images of what a "home" should be and look like.

Involvement in the planning of an environment can involve different degrees of user participation, ranging from (1) the creation of forms and objects themselves, to (2) the selection and arrangement of forms and objects that are provided, to (3) a choice between alternative plans that are complete in themselves, to (4) feedback describing actual and desired activities, attitudes, and images, to (5) no choice at all. In a laboratory simulation study involving the use of scale models of a dormitory room environment, Abe Wandersman and I attempted to explore the effects of the latter three types of participation on user satisfaction. We felt that a field experimental approach to answering these questions is highly desirable but that laboratory simulations such as the one described below are helpful when used in conjunction with and to supplement field research. The realism of the simulation was heightened by performing the study in a departmental design studio. Subjects were told that the study was done in cooperation with the architect and housing office who were in the process of building new dormitories.

The effect of different types of participation in planning the environment on user satisfaction with the environment was experimentally investigated by comparing the effects of three different types of participation in the planning of a dormitory room, using a scale model. The three types of participation were: (1) *self-planning,* in which subjects generated alternative plans and chose a preferred one; (2) *choice,* in which subjects selected from a number of given room arrangements; and (3) *no participation,* in which subjects simply rated a dormitory room planned by others.

Eighty-five undergraduate students who lived in the dormitories at Cornell University participated in the study. There were forty-four males and forty-one females, including fifty-three freshmen, twenty-seven sophomores, and five juniors. Thirty-seven of the persons were in the self-planning condition, twenty-four in the choice condition, and twenty-four in the no-participation condition. Names were selected in a random fashion from the campus telephone directory, and approximately 80 percent of those contacted agreed to participate.

Persons in the self-planning condition were presented with a wide variety of one-inch scale furniture in an empty dormitory room. The furniture designs were selected from interior design furnishing catalogs specializing in both dormitory and other interior furnishings, and provided a wide range of furnishings including room-size rugs, shag carpets, beds with integral storage space, couches, lounge chairs, and wall units that contained a folding bed, a dresser, and a desk. Soft seating was simulated by the use of model furniture made from clay and painted a variety of colors. More traditional "stick" dormitory furniture was made from balsa wood. Each person was told to design a room arrangement they would like to live in using the furniture provided. Each person then created alternative room designs (both mentally and in arranging the model) and finally chose one of their own designs.

Persons in the choice condition were presented with two room designs, which were selected from among the rooms designed by students earlier in the self-planning condition, and they were asked which room they preferred to live in. Students in the no-participation condition were shown one room design. Each person was matched with another person in the choice condition and thus received the same room that the choice person had chosen.

All students noted their satisfaction with the room layout by indicating the degree of imagined satisfaction with living in the room and evaluating its aesthetic value and suitability for various activities, such as studying, socializing, and relaxing. They also ranked the room in comparison with dormitory rooms already in existence at Cornell and answered questions about the participation process.

An important finding was that there were relatively few differences between the self-planned and choice conditions, although both of these differed on most of the questions from the no-participation condition. In general, these results suggest that having some degree of control over one's proximate environment is important, but it may not make a tremendous difference whether one actually generates the alternatives oneself or merely chooses among alternatives, at least in terms of subjective reactions to the physical environment.

Students in both the self-planned and choice conditions reported they would like living in the room significantly more than did students in the no-participation condition, but the only significant differences between the self-planning and choice groups was that the self-planning students rated the room as more flexible than did the choice students.

There were no differences among the three experimental groups' rating of the suitability of the room for various activities, but there were some differences related to the image of the room, particularly its appearance and individuality. Both the choice and self-planning students rated the room significantly higher on appearance and individuality than did the students in the no-participation condition. Similarly, although there were no significant differences between the self-planning and choice conditions in students' feelings of control over the environment and the degree to which the room met the students' own needs and values, there were significant differences on these questions between the no-participation conditions and both of the conditions involving some degree of choice.

It was also hypothesized that when a person participates in the planning process, the room is more likely to meet his or her own particular needs and values, as well as enhancing one's feeling of control over the environment. There were no significant differences between the self-planning and choice conditions on student feeling of control over the environment or on the degree to which the room met their own needs and values, but both of these groups differed significantly from the no-participation group. There were significant correlations between meeting one's own needs, and values, and satisfaction and between feelings of control over the environment and satisfaction. These findings suggest that participation is valuable in increasing feelings of control over the environment and one's perception of the environment or reflecting one's needs and values, and these, in turn, are positively related to satisfaction with the environment.

When we looked at the effect of the different types of participation on the students' feelings about themselves and about the processes they experienced, some interesting differences among all three conditions emerged. Students in the self-planning condition liked the process more, felt they had significantly more input into the design process, and thought that the architects were more interested in their ideas than did the students in the choice and no-participation conditions. Students in the choice condition differed on these same measures from students in the no-participation condition but to a lesser extent than those in the self-planning condition.

Although there were no significant differences among the three participation conditions in making the students feel important, students in both the self-planning and choice conditions felt significantly less alienated and anonymous than did students in the no-participation condition. Students in the self-planning condition felt more creative than those in the other two conditions, and students in both self-planning and choice reported feeling these processes made them feel more creative, responsible, and helpful than did students in the no-participation condition. The students in the self-planning and choice conditions generally did not feel that their participation had been difficult or that they lacked the expertise to participate in the ways they had.

In order to get a direct measure of students' reaction to different types of participation, all the students were asked to rank four types of user participation (self-planning, self-planning in consultation with expert, choice, and no participation). Eighty-three percent of the students considered the self-planning conditions most favorable.

The results of this study suggest that both self-planning and choice types of participation, which incorporate some measure of control over the design process, increase user satisfaction. The general lack of significant differences between students in the self-planned and choice conditions suggests that the generation of alternatives, at least within the framework provided in this study, may not be necessary for producing user satisfaction with the environment. Yet the fact that the rooms students chose between were designed by peers, who share many of their same values and life-styles, probably contributed to the levels of satisfaction found. The fact that one type of participation, self-planning, made students feel more creative than students who had lesser degrees of control over their environment (choice and no participation) and that students in both the self-planning and choice conditions felt more responsible, helpful, and creative and thought that others were more interested in their well-being, supports the kind of effect found in the Hawthorne studies. Being asked to participate is interpreted as an indication of positive concern on the part of administration or management for employees or residents. The resulting physical environment may be slightly better or worse or the same as one simply given, but its meaning for the occupants, particularly in terms of their own sense of worth and self-esteem, is affected by the means through which it is presented to its users. This is not to say that people will not dislike inadequate and poorly functioning environments but that these effects may be softened if these same people helped create them.

User participation appears to increase user satisfaction for at least three reasons: it enables the user to develop an environment that is more closely suited to his or her needs and values; it increases the user's feelings of control over the environment; and it reduces the feeling of anonymity and communicates to the user a greater degree of concern on the part of management or administration.

The satisfaction of these "needs" is generally viewed as rewarding in itself, yet one of the most salient facts about other types of participation related to planning in our society is that they are associated with financial rewards, power, and prestige. Most of our governors, mayors, city councilmen, and college administrators do not participate in dreary meetings and much fruitless planning for the pure joy of it. They are paid to do it; they are given social recognition for it; and they experience some degree of power and prestige because of it. Yet we somehow expect that poor people (in particular) will find it highly stimulating to engage in the somewhat boring and tedious effort to govern a group of diverse people, as is the case in most public-housing authorities. We should expect, and not be surprised, that community participation often fails. The likelihood of seeing one's hard work pay off in the attainment of a goal takes a tremendous amount of time and energy and often does not occur at all. Some external reward is probably the most efficient means of maintaining participation over time. To achieve long-term community participation, community personnel must be recruited and paid as staff. It is the combination of a job *and* a personal stake in seeing that goals are attained that is proving to be a positive means of enlisting community participation and support. This approach has been used in a tenant management project in St. Louis with very positive results.[19] A number of tenants from the public-housing projects were trained and paid to manage the projects they live in, resulting in improved operating performance, including less vandalism, and new opportunities for the upward mobility of residents.[20]

There is little controversy among most

progressive design firms that the images, activities, and life-styles of users of a proposed environment must be incorporated into whatever design alternatives are generated. The issue seems to be the means or process through which these types of data are best generated and incorporated into the design. Over the last ten to fifteen years, architects and planners have increasingly realized that reliance on their own values and experiences and direct contact with only a few of the potential users of a project (the board of directors and executives, for instance), and not the rank-and-file users (the secretaries), often resulted in design decisions inimical to the goals of the majority of the users. This awareness has led to a broader definition of who their clients actually are. It is also a better way of learning about whole groups of clients that had been represented previously only by others very much unlike them (secretaries by bank presidents, for instance). The answer, for many architects, was found in the tools and procedures of social science research, and particularly in evaluation research. Some ten to fifteen years later, many of the same architects and planners who originally turned to social science research have turned back to what they describe as "direct participation," that is, architects and clients (from bank president to secretary) meeting in small groups over a period of time in intensive sessions to explore the kinds of activities, images, experiences, potential areas of conflict, agreement, and so on that each group has and what the implications of this information are for physical design. This form of "data collection" is generally expensive (time-consuming) in comparison to other types of evaluation research, and so it is worth looking at some of the similarities and differences between these two processes, both of which are designed to result in more habitable environments for actual users.

EVALUATION RESEARCH

In general, evaluation research is one strategy for providing designers of programs or buildings with more reliable and valid feedback than occurs when relying exclusively on intuition and opinion. Ideally, evaluation research is a way to increase the rationality of policy making. With objective information, decision makers should have a better basis for allocating budget resources, moving the program in new directions or strengthening the current paths, or continuing or eliminating the program. The production of "objective" evidence is seen as a way to reduce politicking and self-serving maneuvers that generally accompany decision making.

The increased expenditure in time and money evaluation research requires is important when the outcomes to be evaluated are complex, difficult to observe, and made up of many elements reacting in diverse ways. The decisions that will follow are important and expensive; and evidence is needed to convince other people about the validity of the conclusions.[21] The staff running a program are often extremely knowledgeable about it, but their role tends to make them more optimistic than others less involved in the program, and their criteria for success (administrative convenience perhaps) may be inconsistent with other substantive goals of the program. Good evaluation research takes into account the goals and values of all participants in the setting, not only the program leaders or staff.

In practice, the actual effectiveness of evaluation research has been disappointing. Few examples of important contributions to policy and program can be cited.[22] To a large extent evaluation research has been unsuccessful because its function has been misunderstood. Decisions are made on the basis of values, not on the basis of information. The Vietnam war demonstrated only too clearly that even the most overwhelming statistics can be discounted by those who want to believe something else, evidence of scientific objectivity or outright fraud notwithstanding. As Carol Weiss notes:

> Furthermore, for decision makers, evaluation evidence of outcome is only one input out of many. They must consider a host of other factors, from public receptivity and participant reaction, to costs, availability of staff and facilities, and possible alternatives. Those who look to evaluation to take the politics out of decision making are bound to be disappointed. Within every organization, decisions are reached through negotiation and accommodation, through politics. This is the system we have for attaching *value* to facts. Different actors bring different values and priorities to the decision-making process. Evaluative facts have an impact on collective decisions only to the extent that program effectiveness is perceived as valuable.[23]

Evaluation research can serve several noninformational functions as well, including covert purposes such as postponement, ducking responsibility, public relations, and fulfilling grant requirements. The meanings of each type of function are apparent: a decision maker can use a research project to justify delaying a decision; when different factions with the same organization propose different courses of action, evaluation research, by providing "objective" evidence, can cloak the decision one group has made in the trappings of research; one can initiate research to justify the program to the public or to indicate that the program is continuing only after thorough evaluation; and finally, some grants require program evaluation, and so time and money are spent to collect information that the program directors are not concerned about. Unfortunately, it is often difficult to ferret out the covert purposes of evaluation research before becoming involved in the project. Knowing that they exist, and looking for them during the formulation of the project, is probably the researcher's best means of understanding how he or she may be being used.[24]

This brief description of the purpose of evaluation research indicates that its primary purpose is to collect information useful in making decision making more rational; it is a means of systematically including in the decision-making process the views, values, and goals of those who, for a variety of reasons, might otherwise be ignored. It can also be structured, from its inception, to produce information that will support preconceived views. Its primary characteristic, when applied to environmental design, is that it less often benefits those persons surveyed than similar groups of people who will move into new facilities, but this is a function of most private and governmental housing authorities' reluctance to allocate funds to substantial renovation of existing projects, not problems inherent in the research process. How does this process differ from more "direct participation" processes?

The work by design firms like Arrowstreet

in Cambridge, Massachusetts, and Lawrence Halprin Associates in San Francisco appears to be highly successful because it incorporates user feedback throughout the design process—using a variety of participation techniques ranging from surveys to drawing cognitive maps to following environmental "scores" that guide participants through a predetermined sequence of experiences—which heightens the participants' awareness and elicits opinions, attitudes, and images that the designers use as a basis for physical design. The actual design is done by "experts" who then feed back their work to the user participants for their evaluation and comments.

Whether this is "direct" or "indirect" participation is unclear since users provide opinions and feedback on design, but they generally do not generate design concepts or participate in implementing the design. At the scale of urban design, only a minute percentage of those who will actually experience the final design solution can participate in its development. It is undoubtedly true that those who do participate have a different feeling about the final solution than those who do not, but the final outcome can still be highly satisfactory for nonparticipants because it incorporates elements, experiences, and images they desire, and people generally do not look for the same type of involvement with environments they pass through as they do in ones they live or work in.

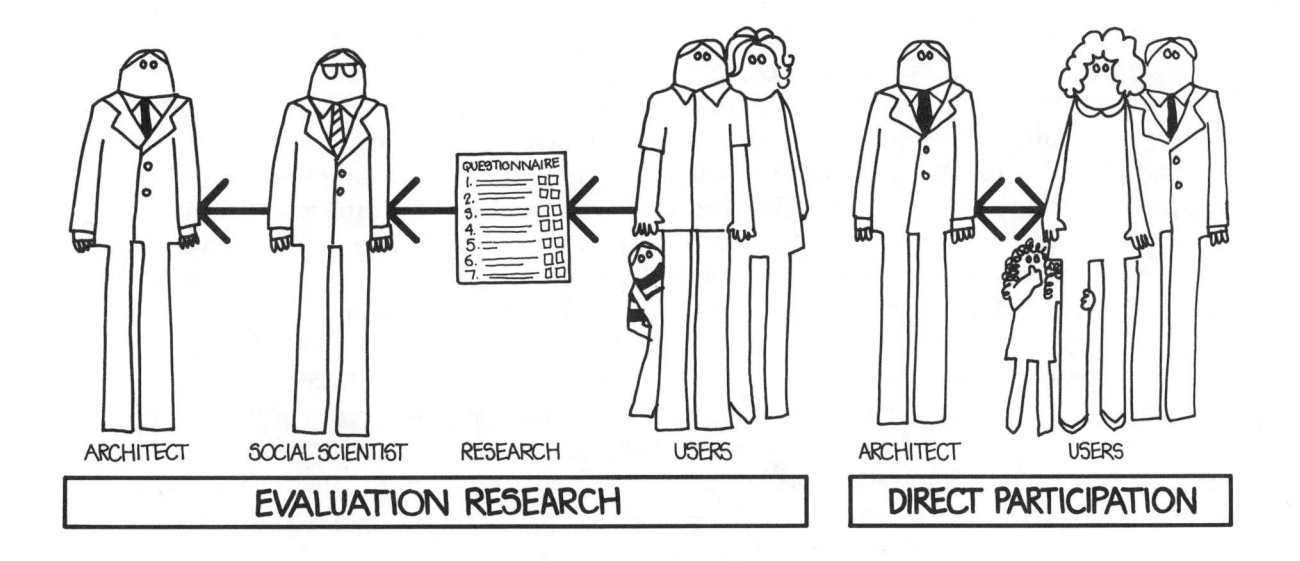

In a basic sense, participatory design makes the same assumption as survey research: by drawing a representative sample of users and eliciting information from them about their desired images, life-styles, and activities, one tries to make valid inferences about how similar users, who have not had the opportunity to participate in the planning sessions, would feel about the same issues. The major difference, and justification, for the direct participation process over some form of systematic evaluation research usually hinges on the concept of "better input," although Christopher Alexander and his group have been more explicit about viewing user participation as an inherently good and beneficial process.

The assumption generally is that no survey can elicit the more deeply held and less conscious attitudes, beliefs, and values that are elicited through a variety of techniques in intensive group sessions over a period of time. This is probably true, but it makes the false assumption that evaluation research relies solely on the brief interview or questionnaire. In-depth unstructured interviews, casual and systematic observation, key informants, archival data, and event sampling are only a few of the techniques that can be used in a thorough evaluation study. One can structure the data collection to elicit the kinds of data one wants.

What seems to be the primary distinction between evaluation research and "direct participation" processes involving groups of potential users in intensive sessions is not "better input" but the increased possibility of two-way communication and the feeling of creativeness and control among participants in the latter process. Evaluation researchers generally do not share their own values and goals with the informants. In contrast, the "direct participation" process is characterized as much by information flowing from the architect/planners to the user participants about their own views of good design and desirable solutions as it is by the architects' soliciting information from the user participants. The fact that the physical solutions resulting from much "participatory" design looks uncommonly like other solutions the same architects have generated without user participation and that many of the solutions incorporate elements the design profession values suggests that a primary benefit of direct participation, from the architect's point of view, is the opportunity to "educate" the user participants to his or her own values, not in a dishonest way, but as part of a reciprocal influence process.

The architect also benefits in another personal sense. Historically, architects did not design in isolation from their client. On the contrary, intensive interaction between architect and client occurred, during which the architect explored the client's goals and values, developed preliminary sketches that incorporated these goals and values, showed these to the client, argued for their acceptance, modified them in some ways, brought back new sketches, and so on.

This model of the design process still operates very effectively today with small-scale residential design and other relatively simple design problems. But as the problem becomes more complex and the number of potential users becomes much too large for the architect to interact with on a personal, face-to-face basis, other methods for knowing the clients become necessary. The direct face-to-face interaction that intensive participatory sessions provide seems like a logical means of combining the need for some sort of representative sample (there is no possibility of interacting with all the pedestrians who might walk down a new pedestrian street) and at the same time reinstituting the very personal and rewarding direct contact with the "client" that characterizes the more traditional design process. It is through this direct contact with representative clients that the architect can develop an understanding of the people who will use the design, and the personal contact infuses meaning into data that might otherwise seem of little importance. In a real sense, the direct participation on the part of the architect/planner appears to be a means of increasing his or her acceptance of the user's feedback, which if generated by a process from which he or she is isolated would produce skepticism about its value. If this is really the case, it suggests that the architect or planner must personally participate in the collection of data, regardless of how they are collected, in order to generate trust in and to make the information "come alive." Conducting interviews, making systematic observations, looking through archival data, and coding questionnaires might be as effective a means of producing involvement of the architect with the data as participating in more intensive group sessions using other techniques. It is unlikely that any secondhand report, regardless of its quality or the basis of the information contained within it, will be well used if the persons who must utilize it have not been involved with its development in some way, or at least thoroughly understand the process that led to it.

Does this mean that *some* form of data collection must be generated for each new design project? Probably. Social science research, like all other scientific research, is predicated on the notion of generalizability: what is learned in one situation can be applied to, or will occur in, a similar situation. When the situation is a vacuum tube, as it might be in physics, generalization is not much of a problem. When the situation is an urban neighborhood, it often is a major difficulty. It seems reasonable that there are social processes or human preferences that are stable in different but similar situations, and indeed studies done in different but similar situations often produce similar results. The complexity of any "real world" setting makes it inevitable that every setting will also be unique in some ways. Social science research attempts to uncover processes or principles that can be applied to different but similar settings. In some cases, at least, basic information will already be available, and the only need is to look for aspects of the situation that make it unique or that can be used to provide a context for interpreting data collected from similar settings. In those cases where the need for information is less important than other concerns—attempting to reduce hostility to *any* design that might be generated, for example—then some form of direct participation process that may have as its major function something other than the collection of "better input" may be the most sensible way to approach the problem.

In many cases, particularly in urban contexts where major parts of the user population are poor, black, or in some way disenfranchised, almost any design will be met with suspicion. Such groups have learned from experience that their own values and preferences are rarely, if ever, taken into account in any type of planning. Their experience of information solicited through surveys or "community meetings" is that this type of input is often ignored, and so they may be unwilling to cooperate in what looks like another social scientist's, or government agency's, "know the people" ritual. In these types of situations, direct involvement of representative user groups with architects may be a potentially effective way of combating apathy and suspicion and, in some cases, the only way of collecting information that has any validity.

Yet the basic ingredient for collecting useful information is most likely not the particular process used to collect the information but the absolute confidence by those being asked to participate that (1) something is going to be built and (2) their views will be taken into consideration in final design decisions. In the case of the UDC study, respondents' knowledge that UDC had paid for the study and that staff members were working for the architects who determined what would be built appeared to satisfy at least the second condition. Respondents knew something was going to be built, but they also knew that their ideas and opinions were not likely to result in any changes in their own living conditions (although in some cases it did). Perhaps a third ingredient, and one that overrides the others, is honesty: not promising what you cannot deliver. The firm of Arrowstreet has resolved this aspect of the research relationship by calling its respondents "user consultants." By paying them a nominal fee as "consultants," they avoid promising them any more than that, as consultants, their opinions and recommendations will be taken into account although they may not necessarily be used in the design—as is true of the designer's recommendations to their client.

Another potential effect/benefit of the direct participation process not related to the "better input" assumption is the possibility that the persons participating in the intensive sessions will become "goodwill ambassadors," for both the architects and the sponsoring agency or body. Following something like a two-step flow of communication, the participants may become convinced of certain design concepts (which may be the ones they have learned to appreciate by interacting with the architects) and, in turn, convince their neighbors of the "rightness" of these design concepts. Through this two-step communication process, the number of people who feel they are participating, or at least being represented by people they trust, may be greatly expanded beyond the actual number of people participating in the sessions. Through their contact with friends and neighbors the actual participants may also elicit ideas and opinions that they will incorporate into their own thinking and bring back into the sessions, thus enriching the range of ideas explored in the sessions. Over time, as different design projects occur and different groups of users participate, the general awareness and acceptance of professional design concepts may increase to the point where, from a professional viewpoint, the overall quality of the urban environment will be improved.

This discussion of "direct" and "indirect" participation raises more questions than it answers, but it seems useful to attempt to understand the potential of different processes and their impact on both the quality of design per se and on different groups' acceptance of the design.

Without systematic empirical data the debate over user participation in the design process will continue to be waged passionately and indecisively. Whether the potential effects of user participation (increased satisfaction with the environment, increased feelings of responsibility and control over the environment, less alienation, "better" environments) are significant in the designer's and paying-client's cost-benefit matrix depends largely upon each's philosophy of the purpose of the built environment. Each must ask to what extent the built environment is a means to an end, rather than an end in itself, and to what extent the architect and paying client should be concerned about the built environment's impact on the user's sense of competence, self-esteem, and satisfaction.

REFERENCES

1. C. Alexander, et al., *The Oregon Experiment* (New York: Oxford University Press, 1975).
2. G. Coates, "Action Research and Community Power: A Prospectus for Environmental Change" (unpublished manuscript, Cornell University, 1973). L. Peattie, "Reflections on Advocacy Planning," *Journal of American Institute of Planners* (March 1967).
3. Alexander et al., *Oregon Experiment.*
4. G. Bazan, et al., "Wesleytown Report" (unpublished manuscript. Pennsylvania State University, 1973).
5. B. F. Skinner, *Beyond Freedom and Dignity* (New York: Bantam, 1971).
6. C. Gibb, "Leadership," in G. Lindzey and E. Aronson, eds., *The Handbook of Social Psychology,* 2d ed. (Reading, Mass.: Addison-Wesley Publishing Company, 1968), vol. 4.
7. Ibid.
8. Ibid.
9. H. J. Leavitt, "Some Effects of Certain Communication Patterns on Group Performance," *Journal of Abnormal Social Psychology* 46 (1951): 38-50.
10. Gibb, "Leadership."
11. R. Lippitt, and R. K. White, "The 'Social Climate' of Children's Groups," in R. G. Barker; J. S. Kounin; and H. F. Wright, eds. *Child Behavior and Development* (New York: McGraw-Hill, 1943, cited by Gibb, "Leadership").
12. H. Preston, and R. Heintz, "Effects of Participatory vs. Supervisory Leadership on Group Judgement," cited by Gibb, "Leadership."
13. R. Likert, *New Patterns of Management* (New York: McGraw Hill, 1961, cited by Gibb, "Leadership").
14. F. Haiman, *Group Leadership and Democratic Action* (Boston: Houghton Mifflin, 1950, cited by Gibb, "Leadership").
15. L. Coch and J. French, "Overcoming Resistance to Change," *Human Relations* (1947): 512-532.

16. B. Bass and H. Leavitt, "Some Experiments in Planning and Operating," *Management Science* (1963): 574-585.
17. J. Corbett, "Student-Built Housing as an Alternative to Dormitories," *Environment and Behavior* 5 (1973): 491-504.
18. Educational Facilities Laboratories, *Student Housing* (New York: Educational Facilities Laboratories, 1972).
19. R. Baron, *Tenant Management: A Rationale for a National Demonstration of Management Innovation* (St. Louis, Missouri: McCormack and Associates, 1975).
20. Ibid.
21. C. Weiss, *Evaluation Research: Methods of Assessing Program Effectiveness* (Englewood Cliffs, N.J.: Prentice-Hall, 1972).
22. Ibid.
23. Ibid.
24. Ibid.

6

Vandalism and Crime

> The theory that people respond differently to different attributes of the environment is one to which we all subscribe. An atmosphere of dereliction and neglect evokes misuse and careless, if not willful, destruction by some users, while good maintenance and surfaces of good quality are respected and sometimes cherished.
>
> Colin Ward, *Vandalism*[1]

The physical environment communicates, unintentionally but not inaccurately, attitudes and values of one group toward another. Vandalism is a major expense for most public-housing authorities, as well as for school systems and government. Its relevance for public housing is that it visually reflects a climate of anomie and alienation and reflects the despair and frustration often endemic in large public-housing projects. Designers, government officials, and developers create their own behavioral theories of *why* vandalism occurs, and their designs reflect their theories. The belief that it is a waste of money to provide quality materials because they will only be destroyed often results, ironically, in the construction of very expensive prisonlike buildings, which by their attempted indestructibleness, invite challenges to destroy. Because vandalism is almost epidemic in this country, it is worth taking a closer look at what it is and is not and how it is related to the environmental message concept.

The word *vandalism* is derived from the Vandals, an east German tribe who invaded Western Europe in the fourth and fifth centuries and eventually sacked Rome in 455.[2] The Vandals were traditionally regarded as the great destroyers of Roman art, civilization, and literature, and their actions were associated with a general bar-

baric ignorance, lack of taste, and lack of sensibility. According to *Oxford English Dictionary,* the term *vandal* was used in 1663 to refer to a "willful or ignorant destroyer of anything beautiful, venerable or worthy of preservation" and has since been broadened to include any reckless, uncultured, or ruthlessly destructive behavior—particularly in connection with works of art. The word *vandalism* was coined in 1794 by an apologist for the French Revolution who, attempting to cast blame for the destruction of works of art during the revolution on its enemies, likened this destruction to the behavior of the original Vandals.[3] The contemporary meaning of vandalism is still given in the dictionary as "ruthless destruction or spoiling of anything beautiful or venerable."

It is unclear when the term *vandalism* was first used to describe destruction of property in general, but the term is now firmly associated with behavior that appears to be without reason. There are assumed to be specific behaviors that can legitimately be called "vandalism." Sociologists concerned with deviance, particularly Erving Goffman and Thomas Szaz in this country and R. D. Laing in England, take what Stanley Cohen has called the *skeptical* approach to the linking of specific behaviors to what are essentially socially defined acts. In Cohen's words:

> Deviance is not a quality inherent in any behaviour or person but rests on society's reaction to certain types of rule-breaking.... One must understand deviance as the product of some sort of transaction that takes place between the rule breaker and the rest of society. Similarly, a "social problem" consists not only of a fixed and given condition but the perception and definition by certain people that this condition poses a threat which is against their interests and that something must be done about it.[4]

Simply stated, the same behaviors are exhibited by different people, and depending on who is engaging in the behavior, the same behavior can be labeled mental illness or spontaneity, malicious damage or youthful energy. Social class, age, sex, frequency, social roles, and the "occasion" influence how any particular behavior may be labeled. Being nude is acceptable in one's own home (bedroom?), on some beaches, and in some nightclubs (for "performers"), but the same state is likely to lead to arrest in a classroom, the library, or church.

Most people, if asked to define acts of vandalism, would describe what has been termed "malicious damage": pouring acid on car roofs; slashing the tires of all the cars in a parking lot; stripping the insulation around water mains; urinating in public telephone receivers; defecating in elevators, hallways, and stairwells; breaking windows of public buildings and housing authorities;

writing on walls; and ripping out plumbing in public lavatories. This "meaningless" destruction of property may be far more understandable than most people would like to accept. More importantly, the fact that such behaviors are labeled criminal, while others are not, accurately reflects our society's underlying values.

Even such "wanton" property destruction is far less devastating, lethal, and expensive than the destruction and attrition of the urban environment by other forces of society, but these are usually labeled "growth" or "progress." The automobile, for example, may be the most destructive environmental force ever known in terms of the number of deaths stemming from its misuse, the amount of space it occupies in our cities to support its continued operation and storage, and the way in which the natural environment has been altered intentionally and unintentionally to accommodate its intrusion or as a consequence of it. Ralph Nader put the issue of environmental violence into perspective when he said:

> The problem of environmental violence is one which should be a major subject of focus because even to this day, I think we will have to admit, pollution is still considered by most people as something that is foul smelling or evil or ugly looking, but is not considered as perhaps one of the two most domestically virulent forms of violence in our society, the other being traffic crashes. Street crimes, burglaries, campus disruptions, don't amount to a fingernail's proportion of the destruction of human beings and their health and their property from traffic crashes and environmental contamination.[5]

This is a rather different way of looking at "vandalism" (property damage). From this broad perspective any property damage that "brings about, or threatens to bring about, physical, psychological, or social damage to persons, groups or societies by the disturbance of the physical environment" is a criminal activity.[6]

It is easy to reject the comparison of pollution and vandalism as similar types of crime if one views vandalism as senseless, irrational, and nonutilitarian while pollution and environmental destruction are viewed as the by-products of rational, utilitarian activities. Vandalism is meaningful, however, from the vandal's perspective and the situation within which his or her activities occur, in the same way that the corporate executive's decision to pollute the environment is meaningful within the framework of a capitalistic society where economic motives are highly valued. Vandalism, unlike industrial pollution or white-collar crime, cannot be explained in terms of the accredited motives of acquiring material gain, so it is described as motiveless. Any other assumption would be threatening.

The willingness of people to define essentially similar behaviors in different ways, depending largely on *who* does it, is well illustrated by "white-collar" crime. Rather than conventional theft by force of burglary, white-collar crime involves violation of job-related trusts, such as kickbacks or embezzlement, which are usually committed by "respectable citizens" of professional stature.[7] White-collar criminals are characterized by their use of rationalizations, which range from unusual circumstances and general irresponsibility to the notion that they are "only borrowing" the item or money involved.[8] What distinguishes white-collar crim-

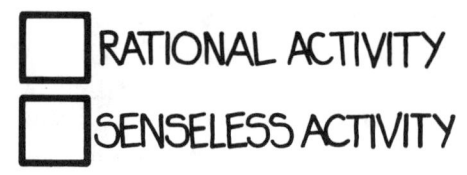

☐ RATIONAL ACTIVITY
☐ SENSELESS ACTIVITY

☐ RATIONAL ACTIVITY
☐ SENSELESS ACTIVITY

inals from most vandals is that society is interested in learning about the motives for white-collar crimes and often bestows a certain amount of status on criminals whose schemes are clever. The motive of personal financial gain that characterizes most white-collar crimes is generally accepted as valid or understandable by society, while the simple destruction of property is defined in different ways, depending on who causes the damage, and when and where it occurs.

General delinquency statistics confirm most of our stereotypes about *who* are delinquents. Far more boys than girls are involved in delinquency; the majority of delinquent children are fourteen years old or more; disproportionately more delinquents are drawn from families of marginal groups on the American scene, including urban-drifting blacks and Spanish-speaking people; and delinquents are disproportionately drawn from the families of lower socioeconomic status.[9] Based on a large sample of apprehended delinquents in the Bronx, John Martin found some significant differences between vandals, as a subgroup of delinquents, compared to delinquents as a whole. Vandals were exclusively boys; the mean age for vandals was 12.94 years compared to the mean age of 14.46 for other delinquents; a slightly higher proportion of whites than nonwhites were vandals; and almost all vandalism involved some type of group effort.[10]

We are, as a society, less aware of how much property damage is ignored or lightly passed over as institutionalized, and legitimized, rule breaking. Stanley Cohen provides an interesting typology of such "acceptable" property destruction, which includes the following categories:

(1) *Ritualism.* On some fixed occasions, such as Halloween and after certain sporting events like the World Series or Super Bowl football game, certain types of property is ritually destroyed, and even encouraged. These acts of destruction are usually labeled "pranks" or exuberance that got a little out of hand, and not as deviant behavior. The police and courts often seem to regard processing of such offenses as a tiresome duty not to be taken seriously by either the officials or the offenders.

(2) *Protection.* Similar to the first condition is the behavior of certain groups who are given something like a collective license by the community to engage in vandalism. Students have been a prime example of such groups, where destruction at year end parties has been labeled "fun" or "letting off steam." Even when punished, the severity of the punishment is seldom as severe as it would be for those of an unprotected group, such as a street corner gang. It is fairly obvious that protection is awarded on a social class basis.

(3) *Play.* Rule-breaking as part of play is less often punished than other forms of deviance because it is somewhat understandable ("that's the way children are") or because the activity is a local tradition or the targets, as derelict houses, are regarded as "fair game." Who breaks what, one what occasion, as noted above, also determines whether the same behavior will be labeled "criminal" or acceptable.

(4) *Writing-off.* These acts of damage are so common, and so infrequently reported, that they contribute very little to the public's stereotype of "vandalism." Graffiti on lavatory walls and names scratched on walls of ancient monuments are common examples. Such defacement or damage is institutionalized in the sense that it is expected. Large supermarkets write off a certain amount of loss from shoplifting and theft by employees as "stock shrinkage."[11]

The central reason for nonenforcement of such criminal infractions is applicable to other types of property theft or destruction: these are some of the safest and most anonymous of offenses. There is no personal complainant, no property to carry or dispose of; detection rates are low, and most damage is not thought worth bothering about; the total cost is considerable (but the individual acts seem trivial). An exception to this state of affairs occurs when the damage involves defacement of religious property and other symbolically sacred property such as war memorials. Attacks on these objects elicit more feelings of anger, fear, and vindictiveness than attacks on the local supermarket.

There is now a clearer understanding that property damage may be motivated by a set of beliefs or ideology in the case of industrial sabotage, but more often the ideological motivation and expressive intent underlying property damage is ignored as a means of undermining the serious intentions of the offenders and the conditions they seek to change. For example, property damage by the Luddites, a group of early nineteenth-century English workmen who destroyed industrial machinery, was originally described as "pointless and frenzied." More recently, Hobshawn has called this type of machine breaking "collective bargaining by riot," because the wrecking implied no special hostility to machines as such but was a means of putting pressure on an employer, particularly to gain wage increases.[12] The employees' sabotage of the Lordstown plant of General Motors was clearly a last-ditch attempt to communicate anger and frustration stemming from alienation from machines to an employer who treated people as simple extensions of machines. A major reason for this type of destruction is the absence of legitimate, and *effective,* means of expressing grievances. It is one means of initiating communication in unresponsive institutional and bureaucratic settings.

Less organized, but similar in intent to industrial sabotage, is vindictive vandalism. It is used to express anger, to settle a grudge, to show that one feels mistreated. According to Prewer breaking a man's window is a much safer way of paying him than punching him in the nose, for example.

> The victim is left with a cold draught, to be followed later by a glazier's bill; and he may remain in complete ignorance as to who has done the deed. The smash itself may be pleasurable, so that this form of revenge is often safe, usually certain and always sweet.[13]

The behavior is meaningful from the vandal's perspective. Ignoring or denying the underlying motivation of the action simply leads to a spiraling chain reaction of recrimination and counter-recrimination.

Deliberate property destruction needs to be distinguished from nonmalicious property damage associated with children's play. Damage caused by hard but legitimate use, damage that occurs when facilities are altered to meet user needs without official sanction, and damage caused by materials easily damaged or placed where they require extra care have been identified by John Zeisel as types of activities that are treated as malicious vandalism but that do not share the same motivation.[14]

The myth of "senselessness" attached to certain types of property damage has not fostered much systematic study of the conditions favorable to it, but the physical and social conditions with which malicious vandalism is associated are not obscure. The property destroyed is more likely to be public than private, largely because of the anonymous nature and symbolic value of public property. The target is depersonalized,

☐ VANDALISM
☐ CREATIVE EXPRESSION

not identified with, and is seen as "theirs" rather than "ours." Property often tends to be derelict, incomplete, or badly kept. Areas of high vandalism also have particular social characteristics. In the case of schools, for example, the following elements have been found associated with large amounts of vandalism: rapid staff turnover; low staff morale; little identification among parents, teachers, and pupils with the school; a record of adverse publicity and a bad reputation; dissatisfaction with the administration; obsolete school apparatus; failure to repair broken equipment and over-crowding—*all of which were interpreted as a lack of interest by the school administration in the students' welfare.*[15]

These same characteristics, and the same interpretations of these environmental messages, obviously apply to a very large number of public-housing developments. The physical environment supports and validates the participants' view of the administrators as not caring about them. Casual property destruction is essentially the only means of effective communication, intentional or not, that students, teachers, residents, or other institutional users have with the owners and administrators who largely determine the conditions under which they learn, live, or work.

College dormitories, like schools and much public housing, are plagued with problems of theft and vandalism. Dormitory residents differ greatly from public-housing residents in numerous ways, but they share the fact that they are living in facilities designed and managed by others for "their own good." College administrators have attributed property damage and theft in dormitories to factors ranging from coed facilities to inadequate maintenance. It is impossible to devise a strategy for changing a behavior or the use and treatment of a facility without knowing why it is being treated or used in a particular way, yet college administrators, school officials, and public-housing managers have made no real attempt to understand the motivation underlying these behaviors in their own settings.

In a study that utilized three dormitories representative of those built since 1960, Jean Shorett explained some of the ways college students rationalized their "criminal" behavior. Twenty-seven administrative and maintenance personnel representing all dormitories were formally interviewed, field notes were recorded after 331 informal conversations with residents, and 50 past residents of one of the dormitories were interviewed by telephone. Of the 355 residents sampled, 308 returned completed structured questionnaires. Informal observations were made almost daily during the study and involved 8,994 separate observations during 210 systematic observation periods in 42 lounge areas.[16]

A major problem was that the available statistics on theft and vandalism were unreliable. Full inventories of institutional equipment occurred only when dormitory officials had first recognized that an item was missing. Students and administrators had different concepts of theft, which led to differences in reporting. The importance of individually identifiable equipment and facilities was demonstrated by the immediate awareness of theft when the portrait of one of the dormitory's namesakes was stolen, whereas recognition of the loss of a single piece of furniture from the lounge was difficult because all pieces looked alike. An estimated third to half of all institutional equipment losses go unreported.[17]

In informal interviews in all dormitories and in questionnaires completed in one dormitory, residents differentiated between two types of loss within the dorms: theft by outsiders and "borrowing" by residents for use within the dormitory. People who had just reported never having *stolen* or helped steal dormitory equipment would volunteer that they had "used it," "rearranged it to their rooms," or "borrowed it" for various lengths of time. Many residents saw in-house use of institutional property as less than theft since the borrower paid for use of the institution and usually intended to return the item. This kind of personal "cost-benefit" analysis also occurs with many motel guests, who feel that for the price they pay they are entitled to take towels, ashtrays, silverware, blankets, sheets, lamps, and even televisions.[18] Forty-two percent of the residents in one dormitory (only one dormitory responded to a formal questionnaire) thought missing furniture was in individual rooms, but only 6 percent claimed to have stolen or helped steal furniture. The concept of "borrowing," rather than "stealing," seemed to account for this discrepancy.

The length of time of personal use ranged from a couch appropriated for weekend guests to lamps kept the entire year. Students appropriated furniture because desirable furniture was not provided or was inconveniently located. Most residents coupled the rationalization of "need" with the idea that their using the equipment caused little harm to other residents. As one student put it: "It's a chair from our study room. Having a single (occupancy room), I have only one chair. This way there's room when a bunch of guys come in. Also, I don't think it hurts anybody. I would put it back if they used it."

The reasons for *not* "borrowing" furniture were equally interesting. Twenty-two percent claimed that they did not need extra equipment, 16 percent did not want the dormitory furniture, and 4 percent said they had never considered taking any items. Only 6 percent claimed that stealing was against their value system.

Much of the furniture taken out of the dormitories was used to supplement bare households off campus. The distinguishing feature between in-house and off-campus losses was the frequency with which the items were returned. Estimates of in-house return rates ranged from 50 to 100 percent. The general consensus was that items appropriated for use within the dormitory were much more often returned than those taken outside the building. No housing administrator had found a way to distinguish these different types of losses.

In addition to the students' obvious disinclination for labeling their behavior "criminal," their motivation for "borrowing" institutional furniture revealed a personal logic and legitimacy for their behavior. Students felt that the dormitories were there to facilitate their goals and activities and that they had the right to modify the environment when the dormitory failed to do this. This kind of modification falls into Zeisel's category of nonmalicious vandalism, which occurs when facilities are altered to meet user needs without official sanction.

The students' appropriation of facilities and their rationalizations for their behavior initiated a vicious cycle: residents who appropriated house and unit lounge lamps maintained that their studying took priority over lounge activity (a convenient logic). Poorer light in the lounges and fewer activities possible within them supported students' rationale for appropriation of the remaining lamps. Students' own perceptions seemed to preclude the possibility of their seeing that their individual actions did indeed have repercussions for other dormitory residents, but this seemed to occur because all the students accepted the *legitimacy* of satisfying individual and small group needs over the development of a sense of community and shared facilities by an entire dormitory. The students' use of lounge areas communicated as well as any other means their individual, not community, orientation. The response of the administrators revealed the "protected" group aspect of this type of theft and vandalism, as well as the "written off" aspect: dormitory officials had come to accept "borrowing" as an inevitable activity, which was generally included in maintenance and operating budgets.

Much of the theft of furniture in dormitories, in contrast to defacement and destruction of property, appeared to be founded in the desire to improve the environment. Theft in this case countered the design and provision of facilities and equipment that did not support the desired life-styles and activities of those using the setting. College administrators need to explore the conditions students see as justifying their behavior. By working with the students' interpretation of acceptable behavior in the setting and their basis for this evaluation, college administrators, or others attempting to provide better services to their clients and reduce the cost of managing and maintaining a facility, at least have a chance to develop policies that may reduce hostility, theft, and property destruction.

Developing rules and regulations pertaining to the use of the physical environment, which increases user control of and responsibility for managing and designing a setting, is no guarantee that malicious damage or theft will occur. It undoubtedly will. Some people will want to test the extent of the administration's commitment to genuinely delegating authority to the actual users. There is a much higher chance of reducing such behaviors when other users want to maintain the facility because they feel it is worth maintaining than when they are told to maintain a facility that they feel deserves to be destroyed.

CRIMES AGAINST PEOPLE

Most of the concern about "crime in the streets" focuses on crimes against people, particularly mugging, rape, and assault. This focus stems, in part, from the much greater fear that personal crimes elicit in people than do property crimes, especially "vandalism." Crimes against property cause discomfort and are expensive but they are not usually as fear inspiring as an attack on one's own person.

The property damage and defacement and the muggings, robberies, and other crimes against people that many living in large, urban housing developments must endure has led to what Sommer has described as a "security state of mind" among residents and housing management.[19] Armed and unarmed guards, barricade like fences, electronic surveillance systems, and supposedly indestructible materials have been tried with equivocal success to deter criminal activity: chain-link fences are ripped apart, guards are intimidated by threats of retaliation from individuals or gangs of teenagers, and electronic systems are expensive to install. Recently human territoriality has been suggested as an alternative means of deterring crime.[20]

TERRITORIALITY

The term *territory* refers to a specific place or area and *territoriality* to the satisfaction of important needs or drives within that area. Characteristic behaviors associated with territoriality include demarcation of the space (that is, space is identified as a territory in such a way that both residents and outsiders can recognize it) and the defense of the space by insiders against outsiders.[21] The concept of territoriality originated in studies of animal behavior, particularly birds.[22] Animals define territorial boundaries, distinguishing their domains from their neighbors' with a variety of markers, including scent as well as visual and auditory cues. Similar types of behavior seem to occur among humans who build fences, plant hedges, and put their names on doors.

The relationship of the concept of territoriality to the deterrence of crime is based on the hypothesis that residents are likely to protect space that they feel belongs to them and over which they have some measure of control from unwanted intrusion. Such areas are in contrast with space that may be close to their dwelling unit but that is considered "public" (it belongs to no particular person or group and is not distinguishable from adjoining spaces). The "defensible space" hypothesis suggests that residents would be unlikely to protect undifferentiated "public" spaces with which they do not identify against unwanted intrusion.

Territorial definition, which may incorporate physical boundaries such as short fences separating adjacent apartments, is largely symbolic. Most markers do not physically prevent movement from one space to another. They discourage unwanted intrusion by emphasizing a space's "belonging" to particular dwelling units and making salient the spatial and legal norms against intruding into someone else's space. Unfortunately, the concept of territorial definition has sometimes been interpreted to mean the construction of physical barriers such as ten-foot high chain-link fences or reliance on electronic surveillance equipment.

The major advantage of using the concept of territoriality in deterrence of crime is that it is inexpensive, employing psychological rather than physical barriers. Casual surveillance of individually identifiable spaces (observation can occur without special effort or "guarding") is integral to this system of control because it allows those who "own" the space to supervise its use and control the activities within it. Awareness that they are being watched puts potential intruders on their guard. They are more likely to either stay away or refrain from committing crimes if they do enter the premises.

It is unclear whether the greatest impact of environmental design on security is in its effect on the number or types of crimes committed or on its improving the "feeling" of security among residents. Research in the field of transportation indicates that what people *believe* is often more controlling than what actually takes place.[23] For example, the President's Commission on Law Enforcement and Administration of Justice found that the perceptions by people that public transport was crime-ridden resulted in a drop-off in public transportation use. In some high-crime areas of Boston and Chicago, for example, almost one-fourth of the respondents to a commission survey reported that they always used cars or taxis at night, rather than public transportation, because of fear or crime. Other research revealed that less than one-half of 1 percent of all passengers using public transit in Chicago were either victims of or witnesses to crime. Yet 70 percent of Chicago transit riders felt that crime was either "very likely" or "somewhat likely" to occur on mass transit vehicles.[24] These studies suggest that objective indexes of criminal activity may be less important to peoples' feelings of security than their perception of the probability that they might be one of the persons constituting the one-half of 1 percent of actual victims.

Part of the UDC study looked at what residents perceived as the key to security problems.[25] This part of the study focused on the types of locations in urban high-rise developments where people felt insecure, what they considered to be effective solutions to crime and vandalism, and what they saw as their own role in the prevention of crime. No measures of actual criminal activity, as indicated by police or housing administration records, were solicited.

Most residents did not think of security as being related to the environment, with the exception of outside lighting. The influence of the development's location on the perception of security was reflected in many residents in low-rise suburban developments interpreting a questionnaire item on security in terms of children's safety: they were anxious about children hurting themselves or getting lost in hills or woods, being hit by cars on the main access road to the development, crawling into a sewer pipe, or falling off a slope while riding a bicycle. Almost all residents in urban high-rise developments interpreted this same item in terms of fear of criminal activity.

Residents felt insecure, in terms of criminal activity, in areas they characterized as a "no-man's land," which were infrequently used and not under the control or surveillance of anyone. Semipublic areas including corridors, elevators, stairwells, laundry rooms, and open parking spaces created anxiety. The three urban UDC developments, Twin Parks 4 and Twin Parks 6 and 8 located in New York City, and Townsend Tower, located in Syracuse, New York, represented very different "defensible space" design characteristics, particularly in terms of the number and location of entrances into the building from the street.

At Twin Parks 4 there was a single, central entrance, which was always locked, a guard in this central lobby, glass doors that provided visual access between the inside and outside, and some symbolic separation of the development from the surrounding community in the form of short concrete bollards located

100 Housing Messages

Figure 6-1
Territorial boundaries are primarily symbolic. Some *ask* people to stay out; others *dare* people to come in.

Vandalism and Crime 101

Figure 6-2
A chain-link fence elicits more hostility than a hedge, and may encourage intrusion from those it is intended to exclude.

on the boundary of the development and the street. A single main entrance permitted guards to effectively control entry into the building. Townsend Tower also had a single entrance with a glass wall providing visual access between the inside and outside, but the absence of a guard stationed in the central lobby undermined the potential effectiveness of the security design.

The lack of territorial definition between the development and the surrounding community in the form of raised steps or hedges or fences did not give residents a sense of territory or clearly indicate to nonresidents where the development's boundaries began. Young children and teenagers who lived near the development hung around in the parking lot and near the lobby, and sometimes they entered the building. Not feeling that any of the outside space was really "theirs," residents said they were reluctant to challenge strangers no matter how suspicious their behavior. At Twin Parks 6 and 8 multiple entrances and generally open design made surveillance, even by guards, extremely difficult: there were not enough guards to patrol all the entrances and stairways where someone could enter, exit, or hide.

From the residents' perspective, guards were the answer to security problems. Even where several guards were present, residents still wanted more. The desire for more guards, however, did not imply respect for the existing ones. Residents were unhappy with the guards' lackadaisical enforcement of rules, their failure to patrol in a consistent manner, and their lack of enthusiasm for protecting the property or people in the housing development.

The guards' performance stemmed from their understanding of the situation. If they diligently enforced regulations or reported violations, they faced possible retaliation from residents or gangs of older children and teenagers. Not surprisingly, their reaction to these pressures was to maintain a low profile. As a result, employment of even several guards was ineffective. The guards did not live in the development or come from the immediately surrounding neighborhood, and there was no reason to assume that they had any personal stake in protecting the building or people. It is unlikely that their salaries were sufficiently large to counteract the very real pressure they faced not to stringently enforce rules or report property damage. Incentives in addition to salary benefits, perhaps relating to personal involvement with the development and its residents via paid resident security guards, may be necessary to alter some of the negative reaction of young residents toward guards, which hinders the guards' effectiveness.

Residents certainly did not view improving security as their responsibility. Oscar Newman and Jane Jacobs have suggested that when residents know one another they are more likely to come to each other's defense and to defend their territories against outsiders.[26] In all UDC developments a large proportion of residents knew twenty or more other residents by sight and at least well enough to casually greet them, and they felt they could distinguish between residents and nonresidents. Few residents had ever actually challenged a stranger themselves or asked the manager to check out a stranger. In the absence of objective data on the number of strangers actually coming into each development, it may be that few persons challenged strangers because the opportunity infrequently occurred or because knowing whether a person is or is not a resident is a necessary but not sufficient condition for challenging someone.

People need moral support if they are to exercise their territorial rights.[27] It is important not only to know one's neighbors casually but to feel that one can *rely* on them to support one's defense of common territory. In the UDC study there was a significant negative correlation between the percentage of residents who had "no good friends" in the development and the percentage who felt "very secure" in the development at night. The correlation was insignificant between the proportion of residents having twenty or more acquaintances and the proportion of residents who felt "very secure." Knowing other residents well, not simply knowing they are neighbors, appeared to be an important influence on one's feeling of security. Semiprivate porches and balconies on paths adjacent to dwelling units facilitate interaction among residents in areas *outside* their apartments. The absence of people interacting socially in interior hallways in high-rise buildings increased the likelihood that a resident would have to challenge a stranger without the physical presence and visible social support of neighbors to rely on.

PERSONALIZATION AND SECURITY

The significance of environmental design related to the deterrence of crime is that it facilitates some types of social organizations over others. The emphasis in the environmental design literature should be on the ways in which people interact, their attitudes toward each other, and the ways in which these attitudes affect their behavior patterns.

Large multifamily housing developments facilitate social isolation and indifference among neighbors, and residents often perceive themselves as respectable but their neighbors as "unsavory characters."[28] Encouraging exterior personalization (painting, decorating, arranging, furnishing, modifying one's semiprivate spaces) may be a potentially useful way of allowing residents to get to know each other indirectly from nonverbal messages communicated through the medium of the physical environment. Exterior personalization provides visual evidence that one's neighbors are concerned enough about their living environment to try to improve it. As noted in chapter 4, what we do to the inside of our homes is known only to ourselves, some friends, and relatives. These efforts to express values, identity, and, in some ways, the feeling of belonging may affect the occupant's own attitudes and those who visit within the dwelling unit, but neighbors have no visible indication of each other's efforts to make personal an impersonal environment.

Exterior personalization may lead to the development of social norms reinforcing improvements in the physical facility when neighbors are encouraged, by the example of their neighbors' efforts, to take pride in their building and neighborhood. As some of the mutual concerns for maintaining and improving one's home become visible, these initially nonverbal messages may provide some incentive for getting to know one's neighbors better and lead to more intensive friendships.

The study by Bush-Brown described in Chapter 4 suggests that exterior personalization in the form of gardens and flower boxes may initiate a chain reaction of more positive social interactions.[29] Neighbors started to talk to one another and to maintain other parts of their block not directly related to the flower gardens. People began using streets as part of their living environment—for chatting with neighbors, for children's play, and for just sitting and watching neighborhood activities.

As noted above, having good friends among one's neighbors appears to be an important influence on one's sense of security. Buildings with personalization in exterior areas, by indicating publicly that particular individuals (their personalization efforts make them less anonymous) live in the building and have taken some trouble to improve it, are less likely to send the message "easy hit" to potential vandals and criminals than buildings whose occupants remain totally anonymous. Involving people in their own protection is the most effective way of increasing security while minimizing its cost.

Universities' dormitory authorities have substantially reduced the costs of damage and theft by increasing student responsibility and control of their own dormitories.[30] Similar policies could be applied to public housing. A customary scheme is to allocate one or two dollars per student per year from the regular maintenance budget. At the end of the year money not spent on maintenance is returned to students who may use it to buy furniture, paint walls, or in other ways make their living environment more pleasant. Frequently, such programs include giving students increased participation in developing rules and operating procedures for their dormitory. The crucial element in using essentially social programs to reduce the incidence of vandalism and theft is allowing the residents to benefit *directly* from their efforts to minimize operating costs. Incorporating savings from maintenance into general funds or higher profits is unlikely to affect residents' willingness to monitor their own and others' behavior.

DESIGN AND POLICY IMPLICATIONS

In summary, encouraging personalization outside the apartment, in addition to personalization within the dwelling unit, may lead to greater use of outside areas and provides nonverbal environmental cues to both neighbors and strangers that residents are proud of and concerned about their building and development. Such cues are important ways in which design features can facilitate social behaviors and attitudes important in increasing residents' sense of security and, hopefully, decreasing the actual amount of undesirable activity. Social programs that increase residents' responsibility for the maintenance and operation of the physical facilities, while passing savings in maintenance costs directly to residents, were suggested as an additional means of improving security at a minimal cost. At the least, physical design should make the employment of guards in high crime areas more effective by minimizing the number of entries into the building and the number of open, public areas that "belong" to no particular residents or group of residents and by providing good territorial definition between the development and surrounding community.

As a final note, it is worthwhile speculating why planners, researchers, and social agencies have expressed so much concern about "lack of community" in low- and moderate-income multifamily housing developments but have paid much less attention to the lack of community among most middle-income groups who desire privacy and isolation from their neighbors. Al Katz has suggested that planners and researchers are simply attempting to employ "sense of community" as an inexpensive control mechanism that middle-income groups can avoid in favor of more expensive electronic surveillance systems, hired doormen, and better mechanical security devices.[31] In other words, it's not the lack of community that bothers society but the expense of dealing with its financial and social consequences. Katz noted that very few planners have dealt with the issue of the decreased individual freedom that is a by-product of "community" and the group norms characterizing cohesive social groups that delineate which behaviors are appropriate and which are not.

Ironically, although attempting to employ a "sense of community" as an inexpensive security device may be genuinely effective in reducing crime and in increasing resident satisfaction, it may be rejected by low-income groups simply because it distinguishes them from the middle-income groups they wish to emulate and who can afford to buy security without sacrificing their social isolation from neighbors. It seems likely that the effectiveness of encouraging "community," through whatever means, as a deterrent to crime will depend on how those faced with essentially no alternative but low-cost social solutions interpret the efforts of planners and researchers to encourage "community" among them. If such efforts are interpreted as social manipulation, without benefits directly accruing to the participants, it is likely such efforts will fail quickly and dramatically.

REFERENCES

1. C. Ward, ed., *Vandalism* (London: The Architectural Press, 1973).
2. Ibid.
3. Ibid.
4. S. Cohen, "Property Destruction: Motives and Meaning," in ibid.
5. R. Nader, "The Professional Responsibility of a Professional Society," *American Institute of Planners Newsletter*, (Nov. 1970), in ibid.
6. G. Hoefnagels, *Environmental Crime* (Amsterdam: Boom Neppel, 1972), in ibid.
7. E. Sutherland, *White Collar Crime* (New York: Holt, 1949).
8. D. Cressey, *Other People's Money: A Study in the Social Psychology of Embezzlement* (Glencoe, Ill.: The Free Press, 1953).
9. J. Martin, *Juvenile Vandalism: A Study of Its Nature and Prevention* (Springfield, Ill.: C. G. Thomas, 1961).
10. Ibid.
11. Cohen, "Property Destruction."
12. E. J. Hobsbawn, "The Machine Breakers! Past and Present," in *Labouring Man* (London: Verdenfeld and Nicholson, 1964), cited by Ward, *Vandalism*.
13. R. Prewer, "Some Observations on Window Smashing," *British Journal of Delinquency* 10 (1959).
14. J. Zeisel, "Designing Out Unintentional School Property Damage: A Checklist," *Man-Environment Interaction: Evaluation and Application*

(Environmental Design Research Association, 1974), 12:173-186.
15. N. Goldman, *A Socio-Psychological Study of School Vandalism* (Syracuse, N.Y.: Syracuse University Research Institute, 1959).
16. J. Shorett, "An Analysis of Theft in an Institutional Setting" (Master's thesis; Cornell University, 1975).
17. F. Roseca, personal communication, ibid.
18. Lasky, M. "One in Three Hotel Guests Is a Towel Thief, Bible Pincher, or Worse," *New York Times*, January 25, 1974.
19. R. Sommer, *Tight Spaces: Hard Architecture and How to Humanize It* (Englewood Cliffs, N.J.: Prentice-Hall, 1974).
20. O. Newman, *Defensible Space* (New York: Macmillan Company, 1972).
21. F. D. Becker, "Delineating Personal Distance and Territoriality," *Environment and Behavior* 3 (1971): 375-381. Also see J. Edney, "Human Territoriality," *Psychological Bulletin* 31 (1974): 959-975.
22. V. C. Wynne-Edwards, *Animal Dispersion in Relation to Social Behavior* (Edinburgh: Oliver and Boyd, 1962). See also K. Lorenz, *On Aggression* (New York: Harcourt, Brace and World, 1966).
23. J. D. Gibson, et al. *The Motion Commotion: Human Factors in Transportation* (NASA-Langley Research Center and Old Dominion University, 1972).
24. Ibid.
25. F. D. Becker, *Design for Living: The Residents View of Multifamily Housing* (Ithaca, N.Y.: Center for Urban Development Research, Cornell University, 1974).
26. J. Jacobs, *The Death and Life of Great American Cities* (New York: Random House, 1961), and Newman, *Defensible Space*.
27. R. Sommer, and F. D. Becker, "Territorial Defense and the Good Neighbor," *Journal of Personality and Social Psychology"* (1969):85-92, and F. D. Becker, "Study of Spatial Markers," *Journal of Personality and Social Psychology* (1973):439-445.
28. C. Ankele and R. Sommer, "The Cheapest Apartment in Town," *Environment and Behavior* 5 (1973): 505-513. See also Becker, *Design for Living*.
29. L. Bush-Brown, *Garden Blocks for Urban America* (New York: Charles Scribner's Sons, 1969).
30. G. Jennings, "Student Damage Control at Central Michigan," *NACURH Review* (April 1972). See also, F. Eigenbrod, "The Effects of Territory and Personality Compatibility on Identity and Security" (Ph.D. diss., University of Michigan, 1969).
31. A. Katz, "Private Space, Public Space, and Defensible Space" (lecture to the Department of Design and Environmental Analysis, N.Y. State College of Human Ecology, Cornell University, Ithaca, New York, October 15, 1974).

7
Children's Play

Those who cannot create will destroy, for the same reason the architect of the sand castle destroys—to experience life as a process, to have acted.

R. Dattner, *Design for Play*[1]

Most planned playgrounds are easily identifiable: iron bars, blacktop, a swing and slide set, and some metal climbing apparatus. We know more about the special requirements of environments for exotic animals in zoos than we do about human environments, including settings for children's play. Through play children develop physical skills and coordination, try out different role possibilities, learn to differentiate themselves from the world around them, and begin to view themselves as effective change agents—capable of controlling as well as being controlled.

To facilitate this type of growth, play settings must provide a wide range of experiences for different-aged children and should encourage some measure of control and active involvement by them. A playground whose major design criterion is that two 350-pound gorillas could not destroy its new set of swings reflects a different perspective for conceptualizing play and ignores the fact that almost all children are much more resourceful and creative than primates, in destructive as well as language capacities.[2]

Most playgrounds can be divided into one of three major types: traditional, contemporary, and adventure. A recent study by a group in the Environmental Psychology Program at the City University of New York explored the different types of activities and user groups associated with each.[3] Traditional playgrounds were characterized by their equipment, which usually included swings, slides, seesaws, and climbing bars; their location, which usually included schools, housing developments, and neighborhood parks; their users, which included children with caretakers (adults or older children and teenagers); and their activities, which centered on the swings. Contemporary playgrounds were characterized by their emphasis on novel forms, textures, and different heights and their sculptured appearance. Children were often accompanied by adults, but the play activities involved a number of different pieces of equipment, among which were slides with bumps, tunnels to caves, and climbing apparatus. Adventure playgrounds were characterized by their absence of specific pieces of equipment. Play material, including wood, nails, rope, and tires, was supplied, and the children could build anything they wanted. The most frequent focus of activities was the "clubhouses," which the kids made themselves. Here children were found talking, listening to music, eating and drinking, doing arts and crafts, and reading. These areas were often highly successful with the older children and teenagers who used them, but parents, particularly working-class and poor parents, sometimes associate these "junk" playgrounds with their being treated as "second-class citizens" and will do anything in their power to have them replaced with the more traditional play equipment they see in playgrounds in middle-class neighborhoods.[4]

Children of different ages and sexes and even the same children over time need a variety of play experiences. Children like swings and slides and will use them, but their activities are limited by the specific types of equipment found in traditional and contemporary playgrounds. Adventure playgrounds where play is stimulated and limited only by the children's imagination and the materials available provide a healthy alternative, but their use may be restricted by cultural stereotypes.[5]

Prevailing social and cultural norms generally encourage boys more than girls to explore, to experiment, to take risks, and to be competitive. Gary Coates and Ellen Bussard found, using a very small sample of low- and moderate-income residents, that girls' activities were much more restricted (by parents) than boys'.[6] Similarly, Clare Cooper-Marcus found that boys were much more frequently observed outside than girls; more girls than boys were observed just walking or wandering through the site; and boys more often than girls utilized objects such as a model airplane, balls, and sticks in their play.[7] Designers need to be aware of and take into account prevailing sex norms, but they do not necessarily have to create designs that rigidly reinforce them.

Play settings are not synonymous with playgrounds. More young children can be accommodated by proportionately fewer planned play facilities depending on the nature of the areas surrounding the housing development. At developments located near woods, hills, or a reservoir, children, particularly older children and boys, will play in these unplanned areas as much as or more so than in the planned ones.[8] In urban areas elevators, burned-out cars, and empty lots provide a variety of experiences and chance to control some aspects of the environment absent in most traditional playgrounds.

In a sense, all areas of a development are

Figure 7-1
Children like to play on traditional play equipment, particularly swings, some of the time. They also need the chance to manipulate materials and create their own environment. Adventure-type playgrounds allow children to extend and test their sense of competence and control.

used for "play." Hard, paved surfaces such as parking lots and paths are used for riding bicycles and tricycles, and wherever there are hills and slopes, these are used for riding, rolling, and sliding. Public areas such as sidewalks and courtyards are a magnet for social activity for a variety of age groups. Developments with front stoops aid social activity by providing a location for adults to supervise children and casually interact with their neighbors. Parking lots and basketball courts are used by teenagers, adults, and older children for social activities, working on cars, and playing basketball. Preschoolers play in the areas around the dwelling unit because adult supervision is convenient. In urban developments children are also found in lobbies, in community rooms, in and around elevators, on stairwells, and in hallways.

What seems so bleak about children's play in urban areas is not the location per se but that most of the children are engaged in passive activities: sitting and standing and watching others or just talking. *Part* of children's daily play activities are normally passive,[9] but in the UDC high-rise developments active play was relatively infrequently observed. The facilities encouraged "hanging out."

In the *Vertical Ghetto,* Richard Moore describes some of the problems of children living in a high-rise building:

> There are no toilet facilities at the ground level at Blackmoor ... like most children he waits until the last minute before attempting to reach his apartment. In his haste to reach his household, he must somehow gain access to the elevator, which may be held up by someone on an upper floor. It may also be necessary for him to use the stairs, since the elevator serves only every third floor.... The disadvantaged child has seen his peers, and perhaps his siblings seek the privacy of the closed elevator for physical relief. This practice may even have the parental support.[10]

Moore goes on to quote a mother who said, "I know it's filthy—but I'd rather see him mess up the elevator than his pants. I'd be willing to bet that the elevator in them terrace apartments stop on every floor. I guess they are more important than we are." Moore also notes that older boys make a game of writing with human excrement and urine on the walls of the elevator: "Although boys everywhere have always done this sort of thing, the slum child seems so completely lacking in any feeling of loyalty to his structural home that he will urinate within the confines of its walls, on his own landing, and just outside his own family's apartment." Such activities are encouraged by the lack of accessible toilets and become a form of communication, perhaps unconscious in young children but reflecting their parents' more clearly expressed distrust and dislike of their living environment and the housing authority that created it. In an environment lacking challenging planned play facilities, the mechanical responsiveness and potential danger of elevators communicates a challenge and excitement that is difficult for children to ignore. Most parents cannot accompany their children every time they go outside, so children are inevitably forced to use the elevators on their own. The heavy use of elevators as a transportation device, in combination with their use as a piece of play equipment, almost guarantees that the eleva-

Figure 7-2
Designed play areas for children of different ages are necessary, but younger children need space to play right outside the apartment where parental supervision is possible.

tor in high-rise buildings will be overused and misused.

Children prefer equipment that is responsive to their input (it can be pushed higher or faster or manipulated in some way).[11] Static "architectural" play forms are the least used. In the UDC study, swings accounted for only 14 percent of the total amount of play equipment but received 46 percent of the total amount of use. In contrast, the climbing apparatus, which accounted for 39 percent of the play equipment, received only 5 percent of the total amount of use. Slides and sand were the next most popular pieces of equipment, and monkey bars, seesaws, and the basketball court received the remainder. Older children liked larger and more challenging slides, although parents become concerned when smaller children attempted to use facilities more appropriate for older children. Installing equipment not designed for smaller children (the first step to a slide is beyond the reach of a three-year-old, for instance) or equipment separated by age groups are two possible ways of dealing with this concern.

Designated play equipment and areas often are boring and unchallenging for children between five and ten years old and too challenging for toddlers. In essence, designated play areas serve no age group well. Older children's activities are displaced to stairwells, elevators, porches, and paths located throughout the entire development. Parents with children may accept the noise generated by children's play as inevitable, but persons without children can have a difficult time adjusting to it. Well-planned age-appropriate play facilities are as important to families *without* children as they are to children and their parents.

In some cases a "time territory" in which different-aged groups use planned play facilities at different times of the day will evolve spontaneously from natural activity cycles, but the problem of unsuitable equipment remains unsolved.[12] In the absence of appropriately challenging play equipment, children are ingenious in creating their own: "Swings become hanging battering rams for an exciting and noisy battle; children with nerves of steel play swing-the-swing-around-the-top-in-a-full-circle. Seesaws make excellent catapults and are great for the jump-off-while-your-partner-is-up-in-the-air-game."[13]

"Found" play occurs in and on facilities, equipment, or spaces whose primary function is not play related but which children *use* for play. The environmental message conveyed by these areas or facilities is often contradictory for children: a space seems to be particularly suited for ball games, yet the management forbids walking on the grass. Different concepts of function ("seeing" versus "using") underlie the contradiction. Despite signs, fines, and admonitions, children commonly use unintended areas for play. Spaces between buildings and solid walls are used for ball games; paved paths and parking lots become bicycle superhighways; dirt is dug up; poles are climbed. Children ingeniously adapt their activities to the restrictions of the setting by using a whiffle ball instead of a softball.

One management response to such adaptations is to create restrictions on activities ("Keep off the grass", "No ball playing", "No bicycle riding"). Unfortunately (for those who created the restrictions), such rules and actual physical barriers are infrequently successful. Chain-link fences can be bent back, wire barriers can be torn down, rules can be ignored. Rules and regulations developed by management are often accepted by adults as necessary for maintaining the appearance of the development, but most children (and they are the ones directly restricted by the policies) are angered by such rules or see them as another obstacle to be challenged or destroyed. Children will simply tear down or push aside fences erected by management that are in their most direct routes to friends' houses, play areas, or schools. Children view their disregard of these restrictions on their freedom as purposeful, rational, and adaptive to dysfunctional environmental barriers.[14] These behaviors are one means of clearly communicating dissatisfaction with the environment's dysfunction. Much less damage would occur if these first symptoms were used to diagnose problems and initiate a series of creative problem-solving sessions with the children.

Having a separate facility for older children and teenagers may reduce some of the conflict among teenagers, younger children, and parents. A teen center would allow teenagers to get together by themselves in their own place, friends would know where to meet each other, and, as one teenager put it (and adult residents agreed), "It would give us something to do instead of causing trouble." According to another teenager, "This way we will have a place to go and stay out of adults' way and the cops can't kick us out!"[15]

As it now stands, teenagers are provided no place of their own and have no place to go, so they "hang out" in outside public areas at night. Management and other adults in the development generally perceive this behavior as undesirable and attempt to move the teenagers out from wherever they are.

114   Housing Messages

Figure 7-3
Children will play ball games whether or not appropriate facilities are provided. The ad hoc location of these ball games creates tension among children, residents, and management.

Children's Play   115

The only alternative for teenagers is their apartment, "owned" by their parents, and generally too small to facilitate groups of teenagers getting together.

UDC residents and teenagers agreed that a teen center needed supervision. The issue here is not really supervision or no supervision but who does the supervising. Persons against the teen center assumed that teenagers themselves would be unable to patrol and take responsibility for what takes place in the building. Some teenagers felt that they were "capable of taking care of ourselves." The qualifications of a supervisor were not based on age or even race necessarily, but rather on his or her ability to set limits and enforce regulations that the users would find meaningful while allowing them to be spontaneous and engage in the kinds of activities they found interesting. As one teenager said, "Someone who understands and can talk to us." Only one teenager thought that the supervisor necessarily had to be an officially designated adult.[16]

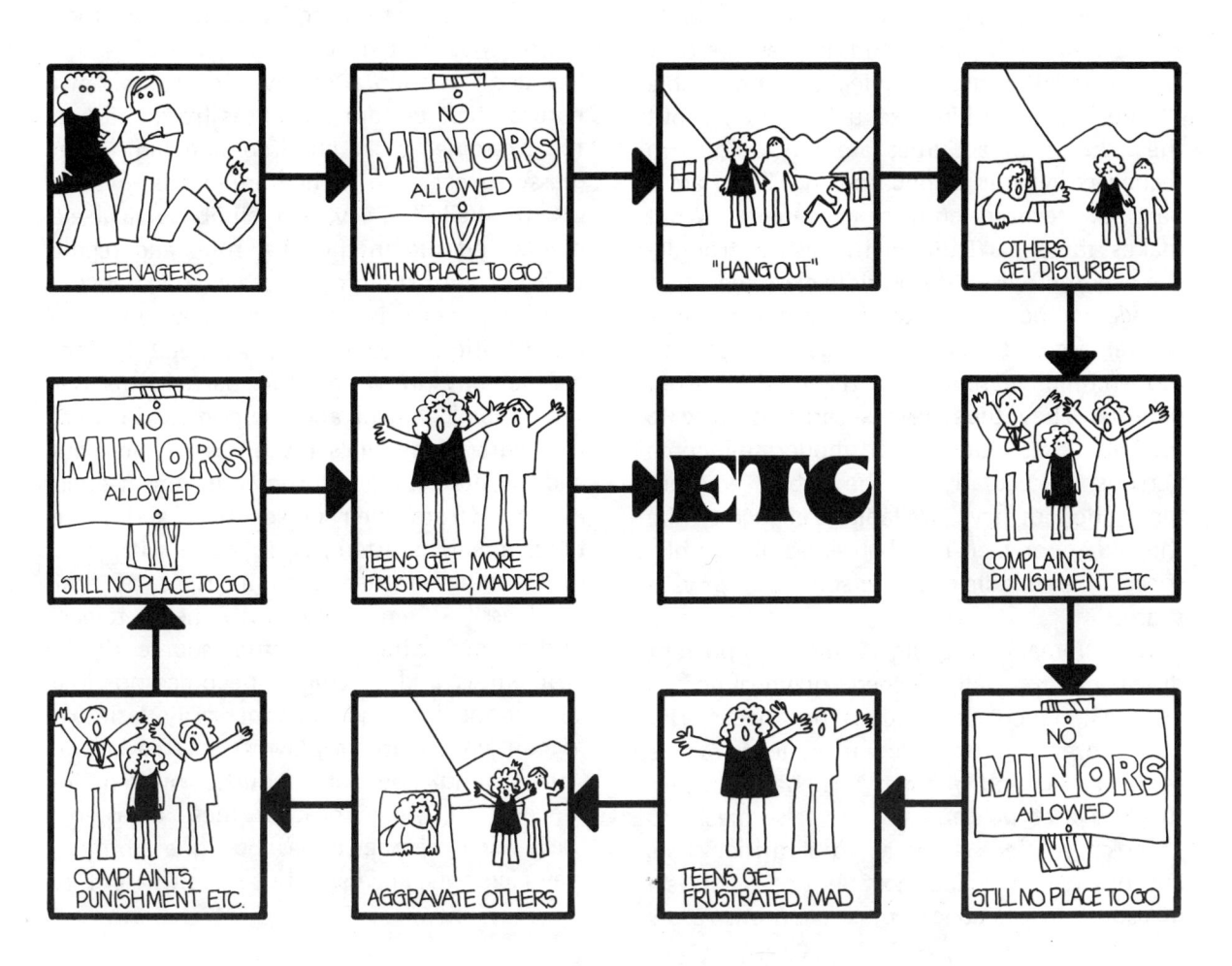

Whatever the location or type of space allocated for a teen center, the supervisor is crucial to its success and must be acceptable to the persons who want to use that space. This person must be paid, and the salary should become a line item in the management's operating budget. Volunteer staffs are successful in the initial stages of the operation when enthusiasm and involvement are high, but some form of permanent staff is necessary over the long run.

It is difficult for public-housing management (and some residents) to contemplate supporting with space and money persons and/or activities they may feel are undesirable ("loitering," drinking, sexual activity), but these kinds of activities are not unique to teenagers living in public housing. They are a part of teenage culture in general. What makes these particular activities so troublesome is their visibility. Middle-class teenagers engage in the same activities, but they have greater access to cars and larger homes with more complete separation of activities from parents. They thus have a series of private settings that low- and moderate-income persons, particularly in the urban environment, do not have available. Teenagers, like the old, poor men in urban areas, use public space like middle-class persons use private space.[17]

In summary, the single most important drawback to well-designed playgrounds is not cost. Good design does not necessarily cost more than poor design, at least over a reasonable period of time.[18] Richard Dattner suggests that we generally use false measures of cost: we look only at total initial costs and not what he calls "cost per use." This is a measure in language most administrators will accept and more accurately describes whether the proposed facility is likely to be worth its cost in terms of its purpose for existing. Inadequately solving a potential problem initially will have repercussions, in costs from damage and maintenance as well as from dissatisfaction and tension, that are often greater than would have been required to solve the initial problem.

Designers and administrators must become more aware of the "environmental messages" the space and facilities convey to children, whether these are intended or not. As Roger Barker has noted, certain types of spaces "seduce" or spontaneously and by their own nature elicit certain responses from children; for example, most children like large open grassy spaces even if they are located in front of city hall.[19] They will climb vertical elements and dig in the dirt, rules and regulations notwithstanding. Rather than labeling what are essentially positive environmental modifications vandalism, we need to look at the way in which the participants perceive their behavior and the context in which it occurs. If people's responses to their dull and uninteresting environments are seen as rational (from their perspective) and sometimes creative attempts to cope with their surroundings rather than as signs of their "badness", then some movement toward finding out what the actual source of the problem is and solving it becomes possible. It is impossible, and not necessarily desirable, to contain children's play to an area labeled "playground" by some adult. Children will use and enjoy the best of these areas, but they must be viewed as but one of many play elements, necessary but not sufficient.

REFERENCES

1. R. Dattner, *Design for Play* (Cambridge, Mass.: The MIT Press, 1969).
2. Ibid.
3. G. Hayword; M. Rothenberg; and R. Beasley, "Children's Play and Urban Playground Environment: The Comparison of Traditional, Contemporary, and Adventure Playground Types," *Environment and Behavior* 6 (1974): 131–168.
4. M. Spivak, "The Political Collapse of a Playground," *Landscape Architecture* 59 (1969): 4.
5. C. Cooper-Marcus, "Children in Residential Areas: Guidelines for Designers," *Landscape Architecture* (October 1974): 272–416. See also Lady Ellen of Hurtwood, *Planning for Play* (London: Thames and Hudson, 1968).
6. G. Coates and E. Bussard, "The Ecology of Children's Out-of-House Activities in a Moderate Density Housing Development," *Man-Environment Interaction: Evaluation and Application* (Environmental Design Research Association, 1974), 12:131–142.
7. C. Cooper-Marcus, "Children's Play Behavior in a Low-Rise, Inner City Housing Development," in *Man-Environment Interaction*, 12:197–211.
8. F. D. Becker, *Design for Living: The Residents View of Multifamily Housing* (Ithaca, N.Y.: Center for Urban Development Research, Cornell University, 1974).
9. W. B. Hole and J. J. Attenburrow, *Houses and People: A Review of User Studies at the Building Research Station* (London: Her Majesty's Stationary Office, 1966).
10. R. Moore, *The Vertical Ghetto: Everyday Life in an Urban Project* (New York: Random House, 1969).
11. Hole and Attenburrow, *Houses and People*.
12. Cooper-Marcus, "Children's Play."
13. Dattner, *Design for Play*.
14. Coates and Bussard, "Ecology."
15. Becker, *Design for Living*.
16. Ibid.
17. F. D. Becker, "A Class-Conscious Evaluation of the Sacramento Mall," *Landscape Architecture* 64 (1973): 448–457.
18. Dattner, *Design for Play*.
19. R. Barker, *Ecological Psychology* (Stanford, Calif.: Stanford University Press, 1968).

8
Housing Management

Through its personal interactions with residents, the quality of maintenance it provides, the rules and regulations it creates, and the manner in which these are enforced, management creates a particular ambience at each development that affects residents' activities and their perception of the entire setting, including its physical facilities. The evidence of concern reflected in superior maintenance or allowing residents to modify their living environments is a form of nonverbal messages—more powerful than verbal pronouncements because they are specific and tangible and speak loudly by themselves.

Local public-housing authorities evolved from the "good government" ethic of the 1920s and 1930s, which stipulated that certain public welfare programs should be run by disinterested laymen who represented the "best of the community" and who would keep these programs "out of politics." Unfortunately, according to a nationwide survey of authority commissioners by Charles Hartman and Gregg Carr, the "best of the community" who serve as authority commissioners generally lack knowledge about and sympathy with the housing programs they administer and the low-income families they serve.[1] Hartman and Carr suggest that the housing authority actually acts as a barrier to expanded and improved housing programs for the poor, primarily because the people who are supposed to represent the poor often find the poor's best interests in conflict with their own.

The conflict of interest, in terms of lifestyle, values, and attitudes, is not surprising in light of the different backgrounds of the commissioners and the residents for whom they set policy. Most housing commissioners are white males in the middle- or upper-middle income ranges, well educated, in either business or a profession, middle-aged or elderly. In contrast, 26 percent of all public-housing families lack a male head of household, over 55 percent of all households in public housing are nonwhite, and only 11 percent of public-housing commissioners have incomes anywhere near the public-housing range (and these are low because these commissioners are retired). The median annual income in public housing nationally is $3,132 for nonelderly households and $1,468 for elderly households, compared with $11,700 for the commissioners. In a survey of 1,891 housing commissioners less than 3 percent had ever lived in public housing and not a single respondent currently lived in public housing.[2]

The persons responsible for initiating, developing, and managing public housing do not represent a cross-section of the community, but they were never intended to. The original notion of citizen boards was elitist and paternalistic. Boards were to be comprised of distinguished community representatives (selected by criteria such as occupation, wealth, and "place in the community") who would have the capacity and desire to represent the multiple interests that the community had in the public-housing program. In the early years of the public-housing program, when public housing primarily served the "submerged middle class" and deliberately excluded the hard-core poor, the assumption that such commissioners could serve the interests of the community, and residents, was tenable. Since the 1950s, when the proportion of minority persons permanently on welfare in public housing began to increase enormously, the assumption has become unviable.

The paternalistic attitude of many commissioners toward residents, which often permeates the entire network of housing authority personnel, has been rejected by large numbers of low-income residents living in public housing who have demanded the right to be independent and to retain their dignity. The increasing responsiveness by many large housing authorities to the demands of the residents for more participation, and from the community for less "trouble" and expense from public housing, were stimulated in part by riots in the 1960s. Insufficient and inadequate housing, and the continued concern by the middle class about the ways in which the evils of the projects were impinging on their own lives, furthered the search for new approaches to providing low-cost housing. Some of the results were joint public-private sponsorship, rent supplements, leasing, rehabilitation, scattered-site development, and a variety of "turnkey" programs in which private developers built projects, which were then turned over to local public-housing authorities.

These programs generally resulted in more satisfaction for low-income families and were more acceptable to the community. They still focused almost exclusively on administrative and financial aspects of housing and neglected the more personal day-to-day relationships and attitudes between residents and housing managers and employees. It is these relationships that greatly affect residents' experience of living in public housing.

Public-housing management is slowly being redefined to accommodate the total range of needs and functions within the public-housing program. Management activities now are more often conceived as an umbrella function to which all other public-housing activities are related and rationalized. From this perspective management's task includes making "public housing projects more livable, more satisfying to the tenants, more economic to operate, less subject to crime, vandalism, and property abuse, more conducive to helping tenants achieve self-sufficiency, self-fulfillment, and upward mobility, and more acceptable to the community as a whole."[3] In 1970 the Environmental Design Research Foundation, under the project title Arrowhead, contracted to identify factors blocking the attainment of these goals as well as policies for attaining them.

The projects included within the Arrowhead study area fulfill most of our stereotyped images of public housing. They were constructed almost thirty-five years ago to serve an isolated class, and the surrounding community had experienced physical and social decline. Of the 1,716 people within the Arrowhead area population, 76 percent of the adults were female, and 39 percent of the total population were preteens and teenagers. The mean income for all residents was $2,864 annually.

The most central and pervasive problem identified—and one that influenced all other problems—was that public housing was an environment suffering from overcontrol by the local housing authority. Instead of providing the opportunity for residents to develop leadership, the environment created and sustained *dependency* in residents through its physical characteristics and management policies. Stemming from most public-housing administration's paternalistic conception of residents and its feelings that the residents are really living in someone else's houses (the "public's?") and therefore must follow certain rules and regulations set down for them by the "public's" representatives (commissioners), residents had become dependent on decisions made by others for them. They looked to others to solve their problems and became resentful when their expectations of necessary services were unfulfilled. The administration recognized the dependent nature of the relationship (but not that they created it) and set forth more rules and regulations for the residents to abide by, removing more decisions from residents' control and increasing their dependency. The study found that residents had no control over approximately 68 percent of the decisions affecting their daily lives. Rules against personalizing one's apartment, the number of guests one can have and the length of time they can remain, what one can put on the walls, and when one has to be quiet are alien to the world of single-family home owners, and abhorrent to those trying to make a home in public housing.

The problem of overcontrol by a central bureaucracy affected on-site management as well as residents and was clearly illustrated by the issue of maintenance. Poor maintenance does not reflect residents' image of respectability, their desire to have their physical environment unambiguously reflect their good citizenship, or their belief that they should receive the same level of services as their middle-class counterparts. Low-income residents, like any other income group, want to feel that the money they are spending on rent is being returned in the form of tangible services and facilities. Poor maintenance is clear evidence that they are not getting what they paid for.

At Arrowhead centralization of management authority had eroded the capacity of management to deliver services at the only level meaningful to residents, namely, their own development. In fact, centralization made on-site management as dependent on a central agency as the residents were dependent on the on-site management. Each's dependency led to mutually destructive relations between management and tenants. Each would accuse the other of not fulfilling some of its responsibilities, and yet neither group was given the opportunity or power to make decisions and set priorities for which they could be held accountable.

The Arrowhead research team recommended that the on-site management be given access *directly* to the resources it required to meet the operating requirements of the development and residents. On-site management needs its own operating budget within which, based on the particular needs and problems of a development, the on-site manager, in conjunction with tenants, can decide which problems have the highest priority and which are secondary. Clear channels of communication and authority need to be established that enable both on-site management and residents to know who is actually responsible for decisions affecting their lives. If residents are asked to provide feedback on existing policy or to help develop new policy, management must demonstrate how their input has been used or the reasons why it has not. Residents' experience is replete with invitations to act in an advisory capacity—with no impact on final decisions.

For housing management to be successful, the relationship between promises made and actions that follow must be clear and consistent. If something is beyond management's control, this should be made clear to residents. It makes little sense to expect residents to accept responsibility for maintaining property or to fulfill lease obligations when management presents a contrary model. Many residents have had primarily negative experiences with landlords and managers and are convinced management does not care about or respect them. Seemingly mundane actions—for example, promptly and courteously answering a complaint or unclogging a toilet—make management's concern and respect *visible* to residents.

Firmness in establishing and enforcing standards of behavior, responsiveness of the management system in meeting individual and group needs, and the encouragement of occupant responsibility for setting personal codes of behavior were found to be good predictors of successful management in an extensive survey of management style.[4] This study analyzed management performance at sixty publicly assisted housing developments serving moderate-income households; in its preliminary report, it found that the most important difference among the developments in predicting success was the characteristics of the occupants: the better-performing projects had a lower proportion of children and more older persons. Developments well stocked with children and teenagers are going to have problems regardless of management policy or style.

Residents' responses to particular rules will vary, but whatever rules do exist should be consistently enforced. Making exceptions to rules creates confusion and mistrust. Residents understand that some rules that restrict personal freedom are necessary for the development as a whole, but rules restricting or prohibiting changing locks on doors, having visitors overnight, having parties after 11 P.M., or building a storage shed or painting a wall seem arbitrary. By explaining the rationale for particular policy decisions, or more basically, sitting down and analyzing with residents problems and strategies for dealing with them, it is more likely that policy and solutions will evolve that satisfy both management and resident requirements. To meet the need for an enclosed backyard space in which young children could play and management's requirement that a tractor-sized lawn mower have access to all lawns, one UDC resident devised a simple folding fence easily set aside on lawn-mowing days. Management exists to protect its investment, and the best way of doing so is to help the residents achieve their own goals.

Pets, and dogs in particular, are a special source of contention. Most managers feel that dogs are a maintenance, health, and social problem. It seems reasonable to exclude dogs, to restrict their size, or to enforce their being leashed. A small damage deposit can be required for the opportunity to have a pet such as a cat or dog to cover any damages they may cause, while other pets, such as fish or birds, would not require special deposits. In Utrecht, Holland, an alternative to private pets is a small zoo with domestic animals like ponies, cows, goats, and rabbits located near large blocks of high-density housing. Children can observe and pet these animals without maintaining them.

Personalization of one's own apartment raises different issues. Management is often concerned about the cost of repainting apartments when the original resident leaves, as well as that the personalization will be in "bad taste." Neither assumption seems warranted. In student dormitories at the University of California at Davis, where inventive personalization policies have been tried and evaluated, the repaint rate was 10 percent—(only one out of ten rooms was repainted by the subsequent occupant). Permitting occupants to paint their own rooms created a substantial savings for the housing administration. It cost $15 to have students paint the rooms themselves, compared to $75 charged by the physical plant office.[5] The same situation prevails at Cornell University. The concern about bad taste seems relevant only in respect to exterior personalization, such as hallways, backyards, and stairwells, where any changes are more visible. Inside the apartment it is the resident who must live with the color of the walls and whether this color is appreciated by one's neighbor is irrelevant. Outside the apartment, sensitivity to neighborhood norms and social pressure is generally effective in controlling modifications unacceptable to surrounding neighbors.

Most residents understand the rationale for policies that allow them to select any room color they want, with no penalty upon leaving if the color can be covered by one coat of paint or charges proportional to the number of additional coats of paint needed. Allowing residents to paint but requiring that they repaint the rooms to their original state before leaving elicits resentment, and they accurately interpret this policy as a means of discouraging personalization.[6] People do not spend time and energy creating something when they know they will have to destroy it.

Despite management's fear that if residents were allowed to paint that all apartments would be a horror of poorly applied clashing colors, some psychological literature suggests that many residents presented with the opportunity of painting their walls, for example, would not actually paint the walls but would consider the opportunity to do so as a positive indication that management was concerned about them and was willing to treat them as responsible individuals.[7] At Cornell University, there are several thousand students in dormitories and painting of rooms is permitted, but only about 400 have taken advantage of the opportunity. Having the opportunity to engage in the behavior but not engaging in it also diminishes the validity of an individual's complaint that he or she cannot live in a place that is unresponsive to his or her own preferences. The apartment's condition becomes a function of what the individual does.

Encouragement by management of occupant repairs and painting has in some cases been negatively correlated with satisfaction with the manager, with the development, and with the condition of the units as rated by the occupants. Sadacca and Isler suggest that occupants view this as an attempt by management to evade its own responsibilities.[8] As noted above, residents want clear evidence that management is providing services and facilities for their rent money, and routine maintenance is very much a part of these services. Encouraging residents to personalize their living environments by improving them substantially in line with their own tastes and values must be disassociated from routine maintenance, which is the management's responsibility. Trying to label routine maintenance as "personalization" is likely to meet with resident hostility, resentment, and resistance.

Physical design that provides a distinct hierarchy of spaces from private through public can increase residents' involvement in maintenance activities and reduce conflict among neighbors.[9] Perin has recently suggested that one criterion for evaluating multi-family housing is the number of rules or arrangements the design requires for successful use.[10] Private yards and facilities do not require elaborate understandings or "rules" clarifying who is responsible for what parcel of undifferentiated space, and therefore the opportunity for conflict is reduced. Given the choice of having their own individual facilities (such as washing machines or private backyards) or the "community" supposedly engendered by shared facilities, residents generally choose the former. Social contacts are important, but residents find other ways of making them: through affinity groups like sewing and sports clubs, religious groups, children's play groups, mutual friends, and casual interaction.

There is a strong belief in many quarters that the number of interrelated financial, social, and psychological problems that plague low-income families require management policies that place at least as much emphasis on the delivery of social services as on the provision of custodial and maintenance services. In the absence of information about resident satisfaction with private management performance, the common assumption is that public-housing management is generally much worse than that found in private developments.

In a study comparing three private and two public-housing developments that ranged in size from 150 to 200 units in Syracuse, New York, Mark Saxer found that the best predictor of satisfaction was not whether the housing was privately or publicly owned and/or managed.[11] It was the management's ability to fulfill what has traditionally been considered management's prime responsibility: prompt and courteous delivery of custodial and maintenance services. The one public-housing manager that was most concerned with the delivery of social services received the lower ratings by residents. Saxer's study does not indicate that the delivery of social services is unimportant. It does suggest that public-housing residents, like any other type of resident, expect to receive prompt and adequate maintenance in return for payment of their rent. Without the delivery of this type of service, which is absolutely basic, all attempts to deliver other secondary services will be relatively ineffective.

We often break into the cycle of events at the wrong place. Residents may be treating their physical spaces badly not because they are socially unstable (although some may be—whether living in public or private developments) but because the physical environments are conveying to them the management's and/or the architect's lack of concern or inability to deal with immediate physical problems. Much public housing, as indicated in chapter 3, was explicitly designed for a temporary group of people and was not intended to accurately reflect people's desired self-image or identity. It was simply a way station. To suggest that the problem with public housing is almost exclusively the residents' and to use poor maintenance or destruction of dilapidated property as evidence of the inhabitants' "badness" is to ignore the enormous sum of money spent every year to repair apartments damaged by pets, parties, and children. By systematically excluding from analysis whole segments of the population, segments that Cohen might call "protected," social scientists have aided in the development of a distorted view of public-housing residents and the type of management they desire and need.

Most people do not passively accept physical environments. They modify them to fit their own life-styles and activities (or destroy or ignore the environments because they are unmodifiable). Although architects often view constructed buildings as finished products, these buildings should be continually evolving in response to changing patterns of user activities. Management should be an active part of this evolutionary process and needs to be made aware of the significance of the physical environment as a symbol of their caring or indifference. Management should begin to construe the physical environment as a very tangible, and potentially effective, tool to help residents meet their perceived needs. This kind of awareness and training is largely foreign to housing management training programs now; most of the educative process is directed instead at fiscal and organizational issues. Little energy is spent on understanding how the physical environment can contribute in tangible ways to everyday problem solving.[12]

We can understand any building only within the context of a particular social system. Management, and the pattern of its relationships with residents, is a major determinant of the social ambience of any housing development. Architects and planners will have to incorporate the management of the facility as part of the total design package

DESIGN FOR TURKEY HILL HOUSING UNIT

in the future. Information about the possibilities inherent in the physical facilities, and about how the architects envision these facilities' being used will need to be developed, along with information about how the space should be programmed over time. Such information will certainly be open to change, but it is necessary to help articulate the design intentions with the actual use of the facilities. For a building to succeed it must, as Phil Thiel has suggested, be viewed as a means to an end, not an end in itself.[13] This cannot occur unless the management of the facility is considered part of the total design.

IT IS THE MANAGER'S RESPONSIBILITY TO HELP THE BUILDING ADAPT TO CHANGING ACTIVITIES AND LIFESTYLE

REFERENCES

1. C. Hartman and G. Carr, "Housing Authorities Reconsidered," *American Institute of Planning Journal* (January, 1969): 10-21.
2. Ibid.
3. Environmental Research and Development Foun-

dation, *Arrowhead Study Final Report* (Cleveland Metropolitan Housing Authority, 1971).

4. R. Sadacca and M. Isler, "Management Performance in Multi-family Housing Development," (working paper 209-4, The Urban Institute, Washington, D.C., 1972).

5. R. Sommer, *Tight Spaces: Hard Architecture and How to Humanize It* (Englewood Cliffs, N.J.: Prentice-Hall, 1974).

6. F. D. Becker, *Design for Living: The Residents' View of Multifamily Housing* (Ithaca, N.Y.: Center for Urban Development Research, Cornell University, 1974).

7. J. W. Brehm, *A Theory of Psychological Reactions* (New York: Academic Press, 1966).

8. Sadacca and Isler, "Management Performance."

9. See Becker, *Design for Living.* See also C. Cooper, "Fenced Backyard—Unfenced Frontyard—Enclosed Porch," *Journal of Housing* 24 (1967): 268-274.

10. C. Perin, "Social Governance and Environmental Design," in *Responding to Social Change*, ed. B. Honikman (Stroudsburg, Pa.: Dowden Hutchinson & Ross, 1975).

11. M. Saxer, "Public Housing Management's Dilemma: Social Service or Maintenance?" (Master's thesis, Cornell University, 1976).

12. W. W. Frank; R. House; and H. Budke, *Management Development Simulation for Housing Directors* (Ithaca, N.Y.: N.Y. State School of Industrial and Labor Relations, Cornell University, 1974).

13. P. Thiel to the author, February 1972.

9
Social Change

Sometimes I become discouraged about the importance of street art in America today. Compared with such critical problems as poverty, crime, racism, and violence, street art seems to be of low priority. Is a concern with art in the midst of intense suffering merely, to use Camus's phrases, "A deceptive luxury, an inconsequential exercise, a meaningless recreation, and justification for a very real oppression"? The answer comes readily when I open my eyes to the drabness of commercial districts, the tawdriness of franchise strips, inhuman public housing, faceless suburban tracts, and the sterility of public buildings.... The entire environment is oppressive and demeaning to the human spirit.

Robert Sommer, *Street Art*[1]

The kinds of physical changes advocated throughout this book—personalizing the inside or outside of one's apartment, upgrading the quality of corridors or lobbies with paint and lighting, painting ethnic murals—may be challenged as relatively insignificant kinds of social change in comparison to the real problems: lower rents, the entire mortgage system, lack of resident control over decisions affecting their lives. These larger issues cannot and should not be avoided, but to argue that such relatively minor physical changes are of little importance is to ignore their highly symbolic character and the very real relationship between the form the physical environment takes and the social system it represents.

The real concern, the only concern, for investigating and trying to understand the physical environment as a medium for communicating values and attitudes is to provide a rationale and data base for making design decisions that will foster and support the diverse human values, expression, and lifestyles of those who inhabit our built environments. The physical environment is a means to an end, not the end itself. By altering the physical environment, even slightly, we begin to alter the social system responsible for it. Such minor changes as allowing residents to personalize the exterior of their apartments, which gives them some measure of control over their own living environment, become a potentially effective means for initiating social change.

Convincing a public-housing administrator to relinquish what seems like a minor degree of his power to the residents themselves sets a precedent for other changes in policy. If residents can paint inside their apartment, why not outside? If they can paint outside, why can't they build a small protective fence? If a small protective fence, why not a storage shed? If this is really their home why shouldn't the residents themselves make decisions regarding appropriate behavior and standards of conduct? Why shouldn't the residents choose their own manager since they are the ones who pay his or her salary? The initial request to change the physical environment, which means changing the locus of power for a particular decision, may appear so minor to the housing authority that it will grant such a change. Subsequent changes may be more difficult to effect, but most people who have begun to experience the exercise of power, no matter how small, want to consolidate their current position and expand their influence. It becomes more difficult to rationalize why residents should not have control over decisions that affect their life.

The best rationale for housing owners, managers, and government housing authorities to relinquish some of their powers is that giving residents responsibility for their own environments makes managing housing much easier and often more profitable; it will also decrease residents' dependency. If management can save thousands of dollars a year on maintenance and damage from malicious vandalism because residents want to protect and maintain a facility from which *they* are the direct recipients of a reduction in the maintenance costs, both groups benefit.

Eventually the increased control of residents may radically alter the structure of the system, economically and politically. St. Louis, for example, has a notorious reputation in the field of public housing. But its housing authority has discovered that the most economical and humane means of managing public housing is to turn it over to tenants themselves.[2] The St. Louis program was set up after a rent strike by residents in 1969. The strike settlement included an agreement that the operation of the development would be turned over to the residents. There are now tenant management corporations, which consist of five-member boards of directors elected by residents that establish policy, rules, and regulations and hire the staff, including the resident manager. Each manager draws a salary and has an operating budget out of which the staff aids are trained. Residents are hired through various manpower programs to keep up the properties and perform security and secretarial tasks. According to residents interviewed, the elevators work now, there is less vandalism, better maintenance, safer streets and apartments, and less drug addiction. The resident manager structure and job program has been supplemented by a cadre of "captains" in each project who are in charge of

125 residents each. The captains serve as a link between residents and managers, handling all day-to-day needs and problems of residents, including enforcing rent collection and facilitating repairs. The impact of permanent on-site managers similar to the other residents was well summed up by one resident who said:

> This development is better now simply because the manager is one of us and lives here. If my lights go off, the manager's lights go off; if the elevator isn't working, the manager has to walk up the stairs just like me. Before we had tenants as managers, the manager was gone to his ranch-style home in the suburbs at 5 o'clock. I never even met one of my managers until last year when a tenant took over.

The encouragement of resident control might also be extended to the physical characteristics of the apartment itself. Residents might be allowed to physically improve their apartments, perhaps within guidelines developed jointly by the residents and management, with the residents benefiting in some direct way from the increase in the property value to the owners that results from their improvements. Residents' rents might be lowered for a period of time, they might get a cash rebate, or even some percentage of the higher rent that might be charged to the next occupant, or they could be given a tax break in the form of a writeoff. This assumes that there is no need for all apartments to be alike physically or in their rent structure and that people will pay extra for improvements as long as the total cost remains within a given price range. This is a means of approximating the "variations on a model" characteristic of vernacular architecture and could stimulate decorative and/or functional modifications that render an impersonal monolithic building more personal and ideosyncratic, while still maintaining the overall impression of quality and stability. The residents would be given a financial incentive for beautifying their surroundings, and the whole community would benefit by the presence of lived-in houses with an individual character.

To maintain the quality of the work undertaken by residents, an arrangement similar to that used by such groups as City Arts Project in New York City, the Chicago Mural groups, and Arrowstreet in Cambridge, Massachusetts, could be developed. Residents work with architects, artists, and interior designers to develop changes that are consistent with residents' tastes, needs, and lifestyles and that also have some degree of acceptance by the design professionals. Work by these groups and others like them suggests that achieving a congruence between community values and professional design values *is* possible if the design professionals are willing to take the time to understand what the community is trying to achieve and what constitutes positive images for it. Intensive weekend workshops can be held in which residents are instructed in building skills by design students or community members with certain building skills, and these persons can supervise the residents as they actually implement the changes themselves. Patterns similar to those now used to sew clothes can be developed for furniture and even certain household products. User participation in this case becomes a matter of choice (select the pattern) and implementation, but the quality of the resultant product is likely to be superior to that attempted by a novice designer. Depending on the backgrounds of the residents, it might even be possible to effect a type of barter economy in which people pay each other in their skills: the carpenter has clothes sewn for her in return for building a cabinet, the outstanding baker has his car tuned up by the auto mechanic in exchange for a German chocolate cake. These are a variety of means for making the social system more responsive to diverse needs through actions essentially related to aspects of people's living environments.

For the architect and designer, the meaning of creativity and originality in design, within the perspective described above, is the ability to adapt residents' or other users' images of home, desired activities, and preferred social relationships to the specific financial and physical limitations of a particular family and site. The designer has tremendous freedom in his or her selection of materials and forms as long as *any* that are created are congruent and supportive of the users' own images of how they want to live or work. Creating forms for their own sake and because of their aesthetic uniqueness is an indulgence of egos that the people who have to live in the forms cannot afford.

Ironically, in some cases the architect or planner trying to involve actual users in developing their own homes, using skills passed down through generations or easily taught to novices and relying on indigenous materials readily and cheaply available, will meet the strongest resistance from poor clients, who stand to benefit most in terms of gaining beautiful and habitable living environments. The poor want what the rich want, even if it's a cheap and bastardized version of it. Hassan Fathy, an Egyptian architect, found that peasant craftsmen were losing traditional skills, thereby denying them to the community, because they associated these skills and building techniques with poverty and backwardness.[3] Although there was no way they could ever afford modern materials such as concrete or even wood, they were unwilling to devote time and energy creating houses that they felt lowered their status. Some American Indians would rather have expensive mobile homes than comfortable and beautiful houses made of adobe.[4] The "faceless suburban tracts" are beautiful to those who can just barely attain them. Before the poor are going to accept modern versions of traditional housing or value their own skills and sensitivities, they are going to have to see the rich and near-rich living in similar buildings and engaging in the same activities.

The development of buildings reflecting diverse life-styles and images of home is predicated on a process of self-selection: different people will select from a number of alternatives those characteristics of a home or apartment that are most salient to them. What one group hates and would not think of living in, another group may consider "home." For self-selection to be a legitimate social strategy for maximizing the satisfaction of a diverse population, viable alternatives must exist within the financial, health, and ability ranges of all segments of the population. In our society the self-selection process is really available only to persons with enough financial resources to select from a number of different *costly* alternatives. Suburban housing is not a practical alternative for people who cannot afford a car to commute to distant jobs. Providing a person with a choice between a rat-infested, unheated, dilapidated house and a public-housing project whose name is a source of embarrassment and ridicule is like providing a person a choice between being beaten to death with rocks or a wooden club. Until we realize that the poor are as diverse in their life-styles and tastes as the rich and want as much variety in their lives, we will continue to create and support environments that are lifeless, impersonal, and degrading.

With a better understanding that those persons whom society deems most socially unacceptable are as vitally concerned with presenting a positive image of themselves and their families as any other income group, our attitude about providing what are mistakenly considered frills in public housing may begin to change, as much for ourselves as for public-housing residents. It is becoming more and more difficult to isolate public housing from the rest of the community. There is, in fact, a trend toward scattered site housing that integrates low-income public housing into the community. There is no reason to avoid what Friedman described as the "social cost" approach to public housing if "social cost" is defined as mutual benefit for all parties. Improving the general appearance of public housing and not stigmatizing its inhabitants as different and separate from the surrounding community is in the interests of public-housing residents, who generally aspire to look like their middle-class counterparts, and to the middle-class community that is concerned about property values lowered by undesirable buildings and neighbors. If increasing resident control of their own decisions in public housing is the best way of maintaining the property values in a middle-class neighborhood, it seems likely that resident control will become acceptable.

Paying greater attention to the meaning of physical objects and environments in terms of the attitudes and values they connote to different groups should also stimulate more scientific inquiry into aspects of the built environment that have often been considered trivial: what do certain materials (brick, wood, steel, concrete, plastic, stone, plaster) mean to different groups; what does the presence or absence of particular types of lighting and lighting fixtures, benches, garbage receptacles, doors, appliances, flooring mean to the people who use them or are affected by their presence or absence? We may begin to know as much about the symbolic aspects of our own ordinary lives as we know about the ordinary lives of the Dogon people in Africa. The kinds of purchases poor people make, which middle-class people view as in poor taste or evidence of inability to manage money, are often made for highly symbolic reasons—conscious or not—as well as for more functional rationalizations.

Money management programs that urge low-income people to forego time-saving devices and "uneconomical" convenience foods in favor of money-saving schemes are based on the faulty assumption that poor people have unused reserves of time. This assumption is based, in turn, on the implicit image of the poor as being idle, lazy, and unemployed. Our society views time as more valuable than money and spends money to purchase machines or machine-made conveniences to save time. The poor are urged to save money by spending time. The "free time" and energy of poverty-stricken housewives are generally limited by considerable demands of family, inadequate housekeeping facilities, and the burden of worry, frustration, and failure.[5]

Within this framework, the decision to use higher-priced convenience foods, for example, can be viewed as a rational choice that allows the housewife to devote herself to other family and household considerations, including social and psychic needs. Convenience foods and labor-saving devices are status symbols. They proclaim to others that one is aware of new devices and can afford to buy them. To shun such status-enhancing products requires a secure status and self-image. Poor persons generally lack this type of status security, and being without status-enhancing products may lead to increased feelings of inadequacy and deprivation. The decision to spend hard-earned savings intended for improvement of an inadequate water facility on a second-hand snowmobile may look like poor money management, and is certainly frustrating to the social worker, but for a society that relies on material possessions for defining status and self-image the purchase is rational. According to Fitchen, this kind of conspicuous consumption may be particularly important for a low-status family:

> The acquisition of a status symbol represents a small but tangible expression of progress toward the parents goal of "providing our children with a better life than we had." As a result of buying the snowmobile, the self-respect of the father-provider is enhanced because, for once, he has been able to provide his family with something other than the barest necessities. The housewife may find that this psychological lift results in smoother family functioning and a general sense of well-being, which outweighs the continued inconvenience of hauling water.[6]

The goal should not be a snowmobile or dune buggy for every family. But these kinds of "inexplicable" purchases, like "senseless" vandalism, point out that to understand behavior we must interpret it within a particular situational context. Much of our behavior is regulated by consideration of status, and physical objects and environments are a significant means of expressing these social values to ourselves and significant others. The objects may often appear mundane, but their meaning within the context of their purchase is seldom so.

Becoming aware of the importance of some of the more mundane objects in our living environments should not be interpreted as support for a deterministic model of behavior. The idea that every aspect of the environment, on a microscale and macroscale, has some specific behavior consequence for the user has some appeal for those seeking direct cause-and-effect relationships. But as noted in the example with the snowmobile, any noticeable change in attitude or behavior is generally influenced by a complex chain of events. The problem with the simple cause-and-effect type of conceptualization is easily illustrated by the attempt to relate crowding to delinquency, poor health, or illegitimate children. In fact there are ten or fifty or more factors that influence behavior. Crowding is generally accompanied by high unemployment, substandard housing, racial prejudice, poor nutrition, and other factors that, when combined, lead to repeated patterns of behavior. It is not possible to isolate and test the effect of these factors in natural situations because situations with high density but unemployment and good nutrition seldom occur naturally. We need to view variables within a specific context. It is much more reasonable to assume that we can understand the significance of a particular building material, for example, when we also know the function of the room, its interior arrangement, the actual users, the circumstances under which they use the room, and the duration of use.

Knowing even this information will not inevitably produce designs that result in either user satisfaction or predictable behaviors. The physical environment can encourage or discourage activities and experiences, but it cannot mandate them.

As accounts by prisoners in isolation cells have revealed, even the most inhumane and complete efforts to eliminate communication are unsuccessful when they counteract a felt need by the users. Such designs are successful in making the unwanted behavior extremely difficult, unpleasant, and as rudimentary as possible—but they seldom eradicate the behavior. Placing chairs in a corner-to-corner arrangement may facilitate casual conversation, but it does not prevent the users from rearranging the furniture to discourage interaction. We must begin to view occupants of environmental settings as active participants and molders of their surroundings, not the passive recipients of others' decisions. Architecture has been described as "an instrument whose central function is to intervene in man's favor. The building has the function of lightening the stress of life.... Although it is true that people are able to adapt to the most unpleasant situations, it is certainly not the architects intention to test people's ingenuity."[7]

While we need to pay more attention to the symbolic meaning of apparently mundane purchases and the possibility that identical objects or environments will have different meanings for different individuals or groups, the assumption that different racial, cultural, or income groups require special living arrangements because of their distinct life-styles may be false, at least within the context of assimilated groups in the United States.

The assumption appears to have been predicated on the fact that most research has not been comparative and has not controlled for variables, such as family size and income. The particular behavior we associate with ethnic groups may be essentially an adaptation to dysfunctional living environments for any large, relatively unwealthy family. Sitting in hallways or on stoops is a reasonable strategy for dealing with small, poorly ventilated, and hot apartments as well as for maintaining social contacts with neighbors in the same plight. Where else can teenagers go to meet their friends and engage in desired activities but outside in public areas when there is no room in the house to gather without adults nearby? What seem like culturally or income-related differences—the popularity of listening to loud stereo music and having parties, sitting outside and talking, or working on cars—may be consequences of particular environmental configurations and economic constraints that make such activities more visible. Large, middle-class families may make the same amount of noise, but better insulated apartments or single-family houses in suburbs render them invisible. It is unclear, at best, that people choose to engage in activities in public that they would not rather do in private if the alternatives were provided.

Stage in life cycle and family composition were much more important variables than race and income affecting satisfaction in the UDC study. UDC residents aspired to and appreciated the same type of housing solutions as any other income or racial groups. I suspect there are greater differences in housing preferences across geographical regions and income groups than there are between different ethnic groups in the same geographical area. High-rise brick apartment buildings typical of New York City probably do not represent a positive image of "home" for black, white or Asian groups in California, Arizona, or New Mexico. Yet the "ranch" style bungalows and flat-roofed houses of the West and Southwest may represent positive images to easterners because their dominant characteristic is that they are detached single-family houses. Within a geographical region it is likely that age, income, and education are better predictors of house type than racial or ethnic identity.

In the final analysis we seem to be faced with a paradox: people are different and they are the same. The clue to the riddle may be that although a tremendous variety of living environments may adequately satisfy basic functional living requirements in terms of the activities and social relationships they facilitate, there are certain ways of expressing social values in these functional arrangements that are more or less congruent with the images different groups have or would like to have of themselves. We need to look beyond functional requirements to the meaning of human values and relationships expressed through the physical environment. The physical environment can become an instrument of social change because by manipulating it one manipulates the underlying social system. Physical and social systems are inextricably intertwined, and the messages communicated nonverbally through the medium of the physical environment are often more convincing, and accurate, than any other form of communication. This is especially true when the opportunity for intense personal interaction between individuals or groups rarely occurs, as is the case in almost all types of institutional settings.

Like any type of communication, the physical environment offers ample opportunities for misunderstanding and the generation of conflict. Attempting to understand the meaning of environmental messages for different groups in specific contexts may lead to the more effective use of the physical environment for broadening understanding, raising self-esteem, and reducing conflict.

REFERENCES

1. R. Sommer, *Street Art* (New York: Links, 1965).
2. P. Delaney, "St. Louis Tests Housing Idea: The Tenants Are in Charge," *New York Times*, June 1, 1975. © 1975 by The New York Times Company. Reprinted by permission.
3. H. Fathy, *Architecture for the Poor* (Chicago: University of Chicago Press, 1973).
4. S. Mensch to the author, April 1976.
5. J. Fitchen, "An Anthropological Perspective on Poverty and Anti-Poverty Programs," *Human Ecology Forum* 5 (1975): 22-24.
6. Ibid.
7. J. M. Fitch, "The Esthetics of Function," *Annals of the New York Academy of Sciences* 127 (1965): 706-714.

Index

Adaptation. *See* Housing, personalization and adaptation
Advocacy planning, 71 (*see also* Participation)
Alexander, C., 71, 83
Appearance. *See* Housing, exterior appearance
Architecture. *See* Vernacular architecture and Built environment
Arrowhead Study, 121-122
Arrowstreet, 82, 86, 131
Authenticity, 9-10

Barker, R., 116
Bass, B., 76
Berlyne, D., 55
Bettelheim, B., 3
Borrowing, 91, 96 (*see also* Theft in dormitories)
Boudon, P., 56
Boyd, R., 12
Brehm, J., 55
Brown, D., 12
Built environment
 expression of cultural values, 7-8, 10-13, 15-19, 33
 expression of organizational and individual values, 9, 13, 16, 18, 23, 25, 35, 40, 42-43, 89, 94-95, 130, 133-134 (*see also* Object language and Personalization)
Bush-Brown, L., 56, 58, 103
Bussard, E., 108

Canter, D., 18
Carr, G., 119
Chaos, result of user participation, 58
Chicago Mural Group, 131
Children. *See* Play
Citizen boards. *See* Management, public housing citizen boards
CityArts Workshop, 131
Coates, G., 108
Cohen, S., 90, 93, 125
Community as crime deterrent, 105 (*see also* Security, social factors)
Competence. *See* Personalization, conceptual framework
Conceptual framework. *See* Personalization

Index

Conflict, different interpretation of physical cues, 2 (*see also* Object language and Meaning)
Coniglio, C., 53-54, 57
Cooper, C., 51 (*see also* Cooper-Marcus, C.)
Cooper-Marcus, C., 18-19, 108
Corbett, J., 76
Cramer, R., 15
Creativity in design, 132

Dattner, R., 107, 116
Delinquency, statistics, 92
Demarcation. *See* Territory, markers
Dependency, 121-122 (*see also* Management)
Design competition. *See* UDC
Design process. *See* Participation
Deviance. *See* Vandalism, skeptical approach to definition
Dickson, W., 4
Dormitory. *See* Theft in dormitories

Eigenbrod, F., 56
Environmental design. *See* Built environment
Environmental messages. *See* Built environment and Object language
Equipment. *See* Play, use of different equipment.

Fathy, H., 132
Fitchen, J., 134
Found spaces. *See* Play, found spaces
French, J., 75
Friedberg, L., 24-25
Friedman, L., 33, 38-39

Gibson, J., 10
Goffman, E., 90
Guards, 102 (*see also* Security)

Haiman, F., 75
Hall, E. T., 2
Halprin, L., 83
Hansen, W., 52
Hartman, C., 119
Hawthorne Study, 4
Hobshawn, E., 93

House form, perception of diversity, 23 (*see also* Built environment)
Housing
 controlling the environment, 33
 exterior appearance, 22 (*see also* Built environment)
 history. *See* Public housing, history
 images of "home-like," 8-10, 12-13, 16-21
 interior size and arrangement, 32-33
 landscaping, 22-23, 25
 legislation
  Housing Act of 1937, 37, 39-40
  New York Tenement House Law of 1867, 38
 maintenance. *See* Management
 management. *See* Management
 personalization and adaptation, 34 (*see also* Personalization)
 play facilities, 30-31 (*see also* Play)
 privacy, 25-30
 restrictions on lifestyle, 31-33
 single-family, 15-21
 storage, 34-35

Identity. *See* Object language and Built environment
Image, making specific, 12 (*see also* Built environment)
Impression formation. *See* Object language and Built environment
Interior space planning, 9 (*see also* Housing)
Isler, M., 124

Jacobs, J., 102
James, W., 5

Katz, A., 105
Kees, W., 1, 4
Kepes, G., 58

Labeling of behavior, 90-91 (*see also* Vandalism)
Laing, R. D., 90
Landscaping. *See* Housing, exterior appearance
Laws. *See* Housing, legislation
Leadership, 73-75 (*see also* Participation)
Leavitt, H., 74, 76
Le Corbusier, 8, 10

Le Pessac, 8, 10, 56
Levittown, 8
Lewin, K., 74
Liebman, T., 43
Lipman, A., 59
Lippitt, R., 74
Live-In program. See UDC
Loose-fit, 58 (see also Personalization)
Lordstown, 94 (see also Sabotage)
Luddites, 93

Maintenance. See Management
Management
  functions, 120-121
  history in public housing, 119-120
  maintenance as communication, 22-23, 119, 122, 125
  part of overall design, 125-126
  public housing citizen boards, 119-120
  rules and regulations
    children's play and teenagers, 113, 116
    personalization, 58-59, 61-62, 64, 123-124
    reducing damage and maintenance costs, 58-59, 64, 124
  by tenants, 80, 130-131
Martin, J., 92
Meaning, hierarchy of levels, 11, 18 (see also Built environment and Object language)
Michelson, W., 15
Moore, R., 110

Nader, R., 91
National Association of Real Estate Boards, 39-40
Newman, O., 59, 102
Nonverbal communication. See Object language and Built environment

Object language, 1-6, 9, 10, 12-13, 125, 134 (see also Built environment and Personalization)
Osmond, H., 56
Overcontrol, 122 (see also Management, functions)

Packard, V., 4-5, 9

Participation
  different types, 73-80
  effects of, 74-75, 77-80, 85-87 (see also Leadership)
  evaluation research versus direct participation, 83-84
  facilitation of, 80-85
Paulsson, G., 7
Perin, C., 54, 124
Personalization
  characteristics, 52-54
  conceptual framework, 54-55, 66
  consequences, 56-58, 65 (see also Object language)
  definition, 51
  facilitation and discouragement. See Management, rules and regulations
  function, 51-58, 66 (see also Territory)
  interior versus exterior, 57-58
  systematic research, 52-54, 56-57, 61
  as threat to environmental quality, 58
Pets, 123
Play
  activities, age groups, and location, 30-31, 110, 112
  age-separated facilities, 113 (see also Teen center)
  found space, 113
  in high rise buildings, 110, 112
  rules and regulations. See Management, rules and regulations
  sex differences, 108
  types of playgrounds, 107-108
  use of different equipment, 112-113
Policy. See Management, rules and regulations
Prewer, R., 94
Privacy. See Housing, privacy.
Psychological reactance, 55
Public housing
  definition, 37
  history, 37-40
  similarity to other institutions, 3 (see also Housing and UDC)
Pyron, B., 23

Rainwater, L., 2

Rapoport, A., 7, 12
Riis, J., 38
Roethlisberger, J., 4
Roosevelt Island Design Competition. *See* UDC.
Ruesch, J., 1, 4

Sabotage, 93-94 (*see also* Vandalism)
Sadacca, R., 124
St. Louis Housing Authority, 130
Saxer, M., 125
Security
  function of perception, 99
  increased by personalization, 103-104
  physical factors, 99, 102-104
  social factors, 102-105
Self-concept. *See* Personalization, functions and Object language
Shorett, J., 95
Skinner, B. F., 72
Social organization. *See* Built environment and Object language
Sommer, R., 4, 9, 58, 98, 129
Status. *See* Object language and Built environment
Stevenson, A., 33
Storage. *See* Housing, storage
Strauss, E., 5
Strodbeck, F., 9
Symbol milieu, 7
Symbolism. *See* Built environment and Object language
Szaz, T., 90

Teen center, 113
  supervision of, 115-116
Tenement. *See* Public housing, history

Territory
  as crime deterrent, 98, 102
  definition, 98
  function, 25, 55
  markers, 51, 98 (*see also* Personalization)
Theft in dormitories, 95-97 (*see also* Vandalism)
Thiel, P., 126
Thorne, R., 18

UDC
  achievement, 42-48
  history, 42
  Live-In program, 47
  Roosevelt Island Design Competition, 48-49
  user evaluation research, 48

Vandalism
  as communication, 56, 93-95
  conditions favoring vandalism, 94-95
  different types, 90, 93-94
  skeptical approach to definition, 90-91
Venturi, R., 12
Vernacular architecture, 11-12, 35

Wandersman, A., 77
Ward, C., 89
Weiss, C., 82
Werthman, C., 18
White, R., 54
White, R. K., 75
Whyte, W., 5
Wohlwill, J., 54

Zeisel, J., 94, 96